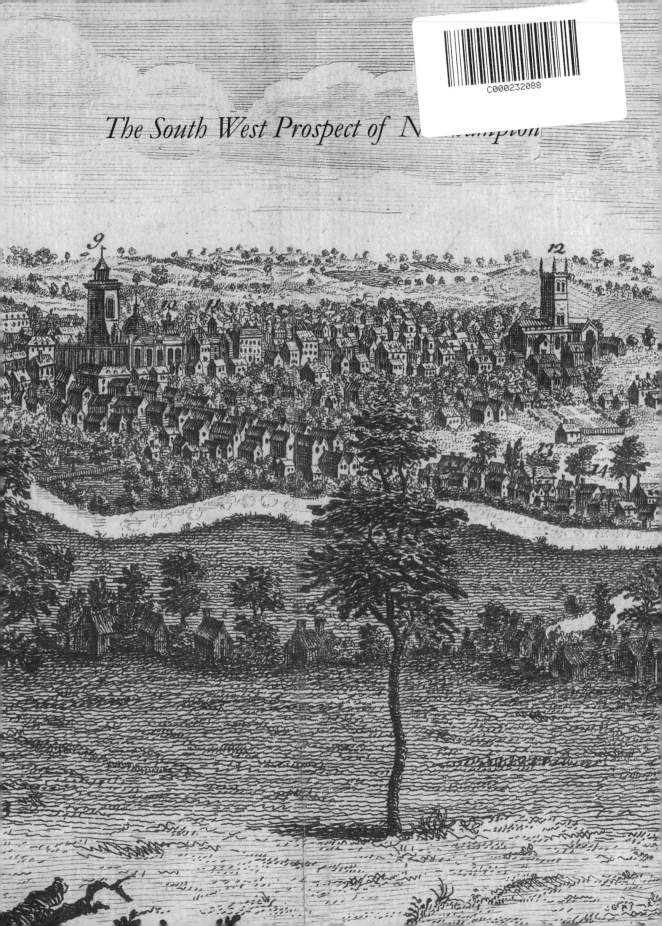

The South West Prospect of Northampton

The River Nene

A Pictorial History

Fotheringhay Church and boating on the river as it is today.

The River Nene

A Pictorial History

Josephine Jeremiah

Phillimore

2003

Published by
PHILLIMORE & CO. LTD,
Shopwyke Manor Barn, Chichester, West Sussex, England

© Josephine Jeremiah, 2003

ISBN 1 86077 257 9

Printed and bound in Great Britain by
THE CROMWELL PRESS LTD
Trowbridge, Wiltshire

To my husband, Ian Jeremiah, for his research and
help in selecting material for this book.

List of Illustrations

Frontispiece: Fotheringhay Church

Acknowledgements

My thanks go to the following for their help in enabling me to compile this book: June Baile, David and Gillian Loader, Valmai Lowe, Northamptonshire Libraries, the Lilian Ream Exhibition Gallery and the Wisbech & Fenland Museum.

Map of River Nene

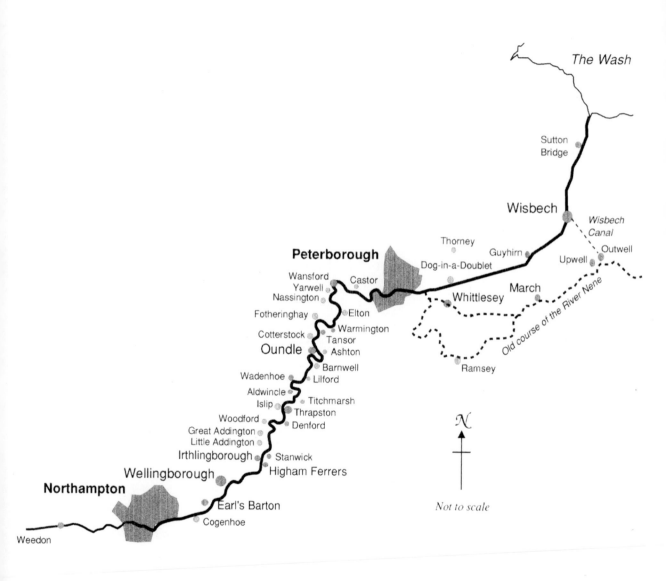

The Wash

Sutton Bridge

Wisbech

Wisbech Canal

Outwell

Upwell

Thorney

Guyhirn

Peterborough

Dog-in-a-Doublet

Wansford

Castor

March

Yarwell

Nassington

Whittlesey

Fotheringhay

Elton

Old course of the River Nene

Warmington

Cotterstock

Tansor

Oundle

Ashton

Barnwell

Ramsey

Wadenhoe

Lilford

Aldwincle

Islip

Titchmarsh

Thrapston

Woodford

Denford

Great Addington

Little Addington

N

Irthlingborough

Stanwick

Wellingborough

Higham Ferrers

Northampton

Earl's Barton

Not to scale

Cogenhoe

Weedon

Introduction

Rising in Northamptonshire, the River Nene flows in a mainly north-easterly direction to The Wash. It passes Northampton, Wellingborough, Thrapston and Oundle, before reaching Peterborough and Wisbech. One of its sources is at **Naseby**, near to the famous Civil War battle site. The other is on the leeward side of Arbury Hill, an ancient hill fort to the west of **Badby**. Situated on a hillside, the village of Badby was originally Badda's Burgh, a fortified place belonging to a Saxon named Badda. This attractive, ironstone village, famed for its bluebell wood, is the starting point of the Nene Way, a long-distance walk covering over 70 miles, following the River Nene, through Northamptonshire, to Wansford near Peterborough.

The country path crosses the infant Nene, before proceeding to **Newnham**. Here, the unusual church tower of St Michael and All Angels is carried by three arches, forming an open porch, where the church bells used to be rung. A feature of this village is 'The Nuttery' in Manor Lane, an old hazelnut orchard, where snowdrops grow in profusion during early spring. A little further away from the river than Newnham, and on the opposite bank, **Little Everdon** is the next settlement downstream. Dating from medieval times, it is the daughter village of **Great Everdon**, a Saxon settlement whose former name, Eferdun, means 'the hill of the wild boar'. Thomas Gray, the poet, is linked with the locality, as his uncle, William Antrobus, was vicar of Everdon in the 18th century. Some say that St Mary's churchyard was the inspiration for Gray's 'Elegy'.

Weedon, several miles downriver, is a larger community comprising Upper and Lower Weedon and Weedon Bec. The Abbey of Bec, in Normandy, once owned land in the vicinity, which accounts for the addition of 'Bec' to the name. In 1803, the Royal Military Depot was constructed at Weedon, which was said to be the furthest point from the sea. It was intended as a refuge for George III, should there be a French invasion. A royal pavilion was built, plus barracks and buildings for powder magazines. The depot was connected to the nearby canal by a short arm, guarded by a portcullis in case of attack.

The Grand Union Canal, the Nene, and the railway are in close proximity at Weedon, with the A5, Roman Britain's famous Watling Street, nearby. Passing under the A5, the stripling river soon skirts the village of **Flore**, renowned for its associations with the Adams family, thought to be the ancestors of two of the Presidents of the United States of America. A couple of miles downstream is **Nether Heyford**, whose claim to fame is its village green, one of the largest in the country, where grazing rights used to be let by 'sale by candle'. A lighted candle would have a pin stuck in it. When the pin fell out, the bidding stopped and the rights went to the highest bidder.

Many watermills were once working along the River Nene between Newnham and Peterborough. Most settlements had one mill, sometimes more, which were used mainly for grinding corn, though some were used for papermaking or fulling cloth. A mill, on the site of Heygate's Mill at Bugbrooke, was mentioned in Domesday Book. Centuries later, corn is still ground here, though the mill is now operated by electricity rather than by water power. Mills between the source of the Nene and Northampton, which have fallen into disuse, include those at Flore, Heyford, Upton and Duston.

A short distance from Heygate's Mill, the Nene is crossed by the M1 before reaching **Kislingbury** on its southern bank. The village is noted for its fine, old, ironstone rectory, dating from the early 18th century, and the cupola-topped, rectory barn, which has over 1,300 nesting places for pigeons. Oliver Cromwell is associated with the district. It is said that his cavalry tethered their mounts in Kislingbury churchyard, a short while before the Battle of Naseby in 1645.

Approaching the town of **Northampton**, the river and the Northampton Arm of the Grand Union Canal run side by side, before the latter enters the Nene at Cotton End. The Nene navigation was completed from Peterborough to Northampton in 1761, while the link with the canal system was made in 1815, by the construction of the Northampton Arm. In the early 19th century, the wharves in Northampton would have been used by both river and canal boats. *Pigot & Co.'s Directory* of 1823-4 noted that Worster & Stubbs Fly Boats left Northampton, every Wednesday and Saturday, for a variety of destinations. These included Wellingborough, Higham Ferrers and Oundle, along the River Nene, as well as places reached by canal.

The huge Carlsberg Brewery is distinctive on the riverside above Northampton's South Bridge, an area well-known for its breweries. The Nene was diverted to allow the construction of this new development. Designed by the Danish architect, Knud Munk, the Carlsberg Brewery was opened in 1974 by Princess Benedikte of Denmark. Downstream of South Bridge, there used to be wharves and timber yards, but the area is now being developed and smart new housing stretches along the left bank of the river.

In the past, Northampton had a Norman castle, but very little remains of it now, except for the castle mound and postern gate. Much of the medieval town was destroyed in the great fire of 1675. However, some fine churches survived. Among them is the church of the Holy Sepulchre. This was built c.1110 by Simon de Senlis, Earl of Northampton, and is notable for its round nave, said to be one of only four in the country. Another impressive Norman church is St Peter's in Marefair. Rebuilt soon after the conflagration, Northampton became, in the words of Daniel Defoe, 'the handsomest and best built town in all this part of England'. The main streets of the town spread out from the focal point of All Saints' Church, which was largely reconstructed after the fire.

1   Over the years, the area around Northampton's South Bridge has been renowned for its breweries. The striking tall building, in the background of this view, was the Crown and Anchor Maltings, built in the latter part of the 1870s. By the turn of the century, the premises were occupied by brewers, Phipps & Co. Before its destruction by fire in the 1970s, the building was used as a warehouse by Brown and Pank. On the right is Bridge Street's *Crown and Anchor* public house, which no longer stands.

Historically, Northampton is known for the Battle of Northampton, which took place in 1460. It was fought between the Lancastrians and the Yorkists, during the Wars of the Roses. Later, the town became famous for the manufacture of boots and shoes. The Central Museum and Art Gallery has a substantial collection of footwear, while the modern sculpture of the Cobbler's Last, near the junction of Abington Street and Fish Street, brings to mind the town's connection with the boot and shoe industry.

The busy thoroughfares of Northampton seem a world away from the peace of the river as it glides past Becket's Park. Just before Northampton Lock, the river divides into two. The right-hand branch runs through the grounds of the Avon Cosmetics factory and rejoins the navigation channel at the site of Nunn Mills. Flowing past Midsummer Meadow, the main channel follows the course dug out at the time of the 1979 Washlands Scheme, when an extensive reservoir was made, further downriver, to hold back floodwater.

Riverside inns are infrequent along the Nene, so the *Britannia Inn*, between Rush Mills Lock and Abington Lock, is noteworthy. There are customer moorings at the inn, but mooring is not allowed on the stretch of river, between Abington Lock and Weston Favell Lock, which borders the Washlands flood storage reservoir. Boats entering this broad reach pass under a barrage gate and leave the flood relief channel under another gate. At Weston Favell Lock, the first guillotine bottom gate is encountered. These lower gates on the Nene locks rise vertically. They have to be left raised, after the lock has been worked. This is to enable flood water to flow straight through the locks, when the river is high. The guillotine gate at Weston Favell is operated by electricity, as are the next two, Clifford Hill Lock and Billing Lock. However, many of the other locks downstream are worked manually.

Clifford Hill, a circular mound, overlooks the River Nene near the lock of the same name. The motte was probably raised to guard a river crossing here. John Clare, Northampton's renowned poet, often visited the spot and it gave him inspiration for lines in one of his poems. A short distance downstream, the flooded gravel pits at Billing Aquadrome provide a large area for recreational use. This includes an extensive caravan site. Between here and Wellingborough, there are a number of lakes alongside the river, which are the result of gravel extraction. These are the habitats of a range of water birds. Billing Mill, near Billing Lock, was working into the 1940s. Later, it became a museum with exhibits connected with milling, but it is now a pub and restaurant.

Villages along this part of the Nene stand well back from the river, on higher ground, to avoid the floods, which, in centuries past, were a feature of the broad river valley. **Cogenhoe**, pronounced 'Cooknoe' by the locals, is situated to the right of Cogenhoe Lock, up a steep slope. It is thought that the name is derived from Cugga, a Saxon owner of the manor, and 'hoe' meaning hill. St Mary's Church, in the neighbouring parish of **Whiston**, stands at the top of a rise, while the tower of All Saints' at **Earls Barton** looks across the Nene from the opposite bank. The latter village is known, not just for its impressive Saxon church, but for its association, over the years, with shoemaking. Both Whiston and Earls Barton give their names to locks on the river, White Mills Lock being between them.

Great Doddington is the next community to Earls Barton, on the same side of the river. In Saxon times, this was 'Dodda's farmstead'. The water mill, which once served the village, stands by Doddington Lock. Its former name of 'Hepdewath Mill' has changed to Hardwater Mill. If legend is to be believed, this was the place to which Thomas à Becket, Archbishop of Canterbury, fled after his trial at Northampton Castle in 1164. Wollaston Lock, a short distance downriver, is also located next to a former mill.

Downstream of Upper Wellingborough Lock, Whitworth's Victoria Mill is still producing flour and dried fruits. Narrowboats once brought imported wheat to the mill from Brentford, along the Grand Union Canal and the Northampton Arm, then down

2 Whitworth's Victoria Mill, Little Irchester. J.B. Whitworth erected this mill, on the banks of the Nene, in 1886. The site had the advantage of the river link with the canal system and the close proximity of the Blisworth, Northampton & Peterborough railway. Victoria Mill was originally driven by steam power, but electricity took the place of steam engines during the 20th century. Narrowboats owned by British Waterways used to trade to Whitworth's between 1948 and 1963. After that, Willow Wren narrowboats took over the grain trade to the mill, until the last boats unloaded in 1969.

the Nene. Even in the 1960s, business was brisk with many pairs of narrowboats supplying the mill. Trading, by water, ceased in 1969, when grain was imported through Tilbury Docks. **Little Irchester**, a small community, stands on the same side of the river as Whitworth's Mill. At the turn of the 20th century, this was a busy place, but the closure of the local iron pits, railway station and river wharf have taken their toll. The Irchester Country Park, situated nearby, is on the site of a former ironstone quarry.

Wellingborough, on the opposite bank, is said to derive its name from the Red Well. This was a medicinal spring, the waters of which were drunk by Charles I and his queen on a visit to the locality in 1626. In the past, before the invention of machine lace, the town was noted for its extensive trade in pillow lace, though it is for the shoe trade that it is most renowned. By the middle of the 19th century, Wellingborough was the third largest producer of boots and shoes in the country. Now, industry in the neighbourhood has diversified. The town expanded during the second half of the 20th century, its population more than doubling. Its centre being some distance from the river, Wellingborough's contact with the Nene is the riverside Embankment, where a flock of swans often gathers. A little way upstream of Lower Wellingborough Lock, the River Ise joins the Nene, while downstream of the lock is the site of a Roman town. An impressive sight between Wellingborough and Higham Ferrers is the brick-built Wellingborough viaduct, erected in the 1850s to carry the Midland railway line across the valley of the Nene. Opened in 1857, it is 350 ft. in extent.

Nearby Ditchford was once a well-known spot on the river for bathing and fishing and even had its own railway station. Ditchford Lock is distinctive for its radial, bottom gate instead of the usual guillotine. Beyond this, the navigation channel used to go under the infamously low Higham Bridge, which could be troublesome for boats, especially during time of flood, because it lacked headroom. This old bridge no longer has to be negotiated, as straightening of the channel has by-passed both bridge and the former Higham Wharf. **Higham Ferrers**, dominated by the tall spire of St Mary's Church, is situated to the east of the river and south of the newly discovered second-century Roman village. In *Whellan's Directory of Northamptonshire* (1849), it was observed that, 'The town is plain and consists of a market-place, and one line of spacious street, nearly a mile in length'. There is much for the present-day visitor to see besides this main street of limestone houses. Features of historic interest include the parish church and nearby Chantry Chapel, the Bede House and the ruins of Chichele College. Higham Ferrers is of literary interest, as the author, H.E. Bates, spent a good deal of his childhood on a family farm near the town. His boyhood memories of life along the River Nene are brought together in his book, *Down the River* (1937), which is illustrated with delightful wood engravings by Agnes Miller Parker.

Past Higham Lock, a bridge, carrying the A6 road 26ft. above the Nene, contrasts with the medieval Irthlingborough Bridge, just downstream of it. The right-angled bend on the river, which comes straight after the old bridge, can make navigation hazardous, when the Nene is in flood. **Irthlingborough**, a small town, noted for its shoe making, lies to the west of the ancient bridge. Its name was recorded in Saxon times as Yrtlingaburg, 'the fortified place of Yrtla's people', and in Domesday Book as Erdinburne. After Irthlingborough Lock, a riverside Youth Club Camp heralds a stretch of the Nene frequently paddled by canoeists. Beyond this lock and Upper Ringstead Lock, the village of **Stanwick** occupies an elevated position on the right-hand bank, while the community of **Little Addington** overlooks the river on its left-hand bank.

Woodford Upper Mill is situated near Lower Ringstead Lock. Formerly used for papermaking, it goes by the name of Willy Watt Mill and is the location of a boat marina. The village of **Great Addington** is to the west of the lock and mill. **Ringstead**, to the east, has a large Pocket Park, close by the river, called Kinewell Lake. Pocket Parks comprise land, which is either owned or rented by a local community. This lake was formerly gravel workings and is the habitat of many types of wildlife. Downriver of this nature reserve, the Nene curves through water meadows towards **Woodford**, where the church of St

Mary is in a prominent position on the river bank. Near the village are three prehistoric burial mounds, which indicate early settlement in the area. Woodford grew in population, when ironstone mining became established in the vicinity, during the second half of the 19th century.

Leaving Woodford Lock, the river meanders on its way to **Denford**, another community located on sloping ground above the Nene. Its name originally meant 'ford in the valley' and is a combination of the Celtic 'den' meaning valley and the Saxon 'ford'. The 13th-century Holy Trinity Church is close to the river, its broach spire adding to the picturesque scene. Here, among the water meadows, is Denford Lock, while, between the river and the Thrapston road the war memorial pays tribute to villagers who fell in the two world wars.

Before Thrapston is reached, the waterway is crossed by the concrete A14 road bridge, then by a brick-built railway viaduct and finally by the narrow stone Thrapston Bridge. In the past, bridges over the Nene were few and far between settlements. A bridging point, such as this, would have been the location for much coming and going so, not surprisingly, **Thrapston**, to the east of the bridge, became a centre of trade for the area. The Nene navigation, completed from Peterborough to Thrapston in 1737, enabled the inhabitants of the neighbourhood to carry on a trade in the exportation of grain, while importing coal, timber and groceries by water. At Thrapston, the church of St James has a stone tablet displaying the stars and stripes, the arms of the Washington family. Sir John Washington, who died at Thrapston in 1688, was the great-great-great-uncle of George Washington, the first American president. Noted for its livestock market, the small town once boasted two railway stations, one on the London and North Western line, the other on the Midland line.

Islip, smaller than Thrapston, lies to the north west of the medieval bridge and gives its name to a mill and a lock on the Nene. The stretch of river, below the lock, is bounded by flooded gravel workings, which are now used by craft of the Middle Nene Sailing Club. Narrowboats and cruisers are to be found at Titchmarsh Mill, the headquarters of the Middle Nene Cruising Club. Titchmarsh Nature Reserve, former sand and gravel workings, is alongside the river just before the mill, while the village of **Titchmarsh**, set on a ridge, is at some distance from the mill and Titchmarsh Lock. Downriver of the lock, the Nene curves around **Aldwincle**. In Saxon, 'wincel' means bend and is likely to have referred to this loop made by the river. **Thorpe Waterville**, on the opposite bank, is closer to the river. An unusual feature of this village is the gable end of an old barn. It has two circular windows, on either side of a jutting-out chimney breast, which is reminiscent of a face.

The river makes another arc before reaching **Wadenhoe**, where a wooded slope, on the left-hand bank, is the background to an idyllic overnight mooring for pleasure craft. The name of the village is thought to derive from Wada, the personal name of a Saxon leader, and 'hoh' meaning headland. Perched on a hillock, the ancient church is reached by

3 Willow pollards are on the right of this view of Denford from the Thrapston Road. The tops of the willows, bordering the river, had been cut off, so that the trees would produce a number of shoots. These would eventually grow into poles, which were harvested to be used in a variety of ways including hurdle fencing and basket making.

a steep path from the riverside. From Wadenhoe Church, the view across the Nene Valley is delightful. In the village below, the gardens of the picturesque *King's Head* stretch to the water's edge, where a good view of boats passing through Wadenhoe Lock may be obtained. Here, the Nene splits into two. The left-hand branch flows towards the charming old mill, while the main channel proceeds to the lock.

Past Wadenhoe, the navigation channel continues to wind through the water meadows towards **Lilford**. To the right, peeping over the trees, is the broach spire of St John the Baptist's Church at **Achurch**. This village is also known as **Thorpe Achurch**. Before Lilford Lock is reached, the river divides into two and flows through beautiful woodland called the Lynches. The striking, stone-built Lilford Bridge, with its fluted pilasters, was erected in 1796. It carries the road to **Pilton**, on the river's left bank. This small community is noted for the cluster of old buildings around its 13th-century church and also for the three-storey Bede House, alternatively called the Old Watch House. The latter has an unusual brick-built shaft on its roof. This looks like a chimney, but has a small window so may have been used as a look-out in bygone times. From Pilton, there is a good view of Lilford Hall and its park on the opposite side of the river.

Upper Barnwell Lock, adjacent to Barnwell Mill, is the next lock downriver. It takes its name from the nearby village of **Barnwell**. Between this lock and Lower Barnwell Lock lies Oundle Marina, a boating centre created from former gravel workings. Oundle is not far from its marina. However, instead of making for the town, the Nene now turns away from it, curving around to Ashton Lock. Here, there are pleasant overnight moorings in the mill stream with the Dragonfly BioMuseum at Ashton Mill close by. The village of **Ashton**, a short distance from the river, is renowned for its World Conker Championship, held annually on the village green. Ashton also has a claim to fame as being one of the last places in the country where the Chequered Skipper butterfly was recorded, before it became extinct in the 1970s. The village pub takes its name from this butterfly.

As the river loops around **Oundle**, the tall spire of St Peter's Church is prominent across the water meadows. The architecture of the parish church is mainly Early English, though some parts are in the Decorated and Perpendicular style. The grey limestone buildings of this historic market town, famous for its public school, are a delight to the eye. The fine town houses, with their Collyweston slate roofs, reflect the prosperity of Oundle, in times past, while 17th-century almshouses and old inns are among other distinctive features. A focal point is the Market Place, from which radiate West Street, New Street, North Street and St Osyth's Lane. In the mid-19th century, there was a market on Thursdays and fairs for horses, sheep and cows were held on 25 February and Whit Monday. Another fair for all sorts of stock and cheese was held on 12 October. By the late 19th century, the latter was a fair for pleasure.

Downstream of Oundle's North Bridge, the Nene flows through meadows to Cotterstock Lock. Nearby **Cotterstock**, on the left bank, has a long history. Settled in Roman times, the village was named in Domesday Book. During the medieval period, one of the six collegiate institutions in Northampton was founded here, while Cotterstock Hall was erected in the 17th century. The squat-towered churches of Cotterstock and **Tansor**, the next community downriver, are situated on the banks of the River Nene, as is Fotheringhay's splendid church with its octagonal lantern tower. Approaching Fotheringhay the river curves around Perio Lock and Perio Mill, skirting Bluebell Lakes, which are more former gravel workings.

Fotheringhay is renowned as the place where Mary, Queen of Scots was beheaded in 1587. However, it had links with royalty well before that event. Edmund de Langley, fifth son of Edward III, started the building of the magnificent collegiate church. When he died in 1402, it was carried on by his son. A future Yorkist king, Richard III, was born at Fotheringhay Castle and his parents were buried in the quire of the collegiate church. The quire and college buildings were pulled down in 1548, at the dissolution of the college, but the adjoining parish church was left intact. Elizabeth I, visiting Fotheringhay in 1573,

4   The Nene navigation, from Peterborough to Oundle's North Bridge, was completed in 1730. The short backwater, which leads up to the former Oundle wharf, is in the background of this old postcard view of North Bridge. Goods such as coal and timber were handled at the wharf, while waterside maltings, once served by water transport, used to be on this length of canalised river. In the foreground is the main channel of the Nene, which flows through North Bridge.

saw the tombs of her ancestors, in the ruined quire, and ordered that they should be reburied within the parish church.

There are pastoral overnight moorings on both sides of Fotheringhay's attractive, stone-built bridge, while the moorings of Elton Boat Club occupy the millstream at Warmington Mill. The disused mill is actually in **Eaglethorpe**, a settlement nearer to the river than its larger neighbour **Warmington**. Eaglethorpe is noted for the circular dovecot at Eaglethorpe Farm and Warmington for its Early English church, dedicated to St Mary the Virgin. Leaving Warmington Lock, the river winds around towards Elton Lock. Elton Mill is situated between the lock and the village of **Elton**. It is a striking building, even in its dereliction, with a jutting-out, timber-clad hoist and numerous boarded-up windows. The author and illustrator, Denys Watkins-Pitchford, alias 'BB', cruised the river in the summer and autumn of 1966. Mooring his hireboat near Elton, for a short time, he found the village delightful. *A Summer on the Nene* (1967) is an evocative account of the time he and his family spent on the waterway.

At Elton, the Nene acts as a boundary between Northamptonshire and present-day Cambridgeshire, though Elton and some other parishes, bordering the Nene downriver, were formerly in the county of Huntingdonshire. Between here and Wansford, the river mainly flows in a northerly direction, winding first around **Nassington**, known for its ancient Prebendal Manor House, and then **Yarwell**, a pretty village with limestone-built cottages. Both villages are on the same side of the river. Nassington has a backwater with moorings for small craft patronising the *Queen's Head*, while the caravan site at Yarwell Mill has riverside moorings for its clientele. Yarwell Lock is adjacent to the mill and holiday site.

The electrically-powered Wansford Lock is the next lock downstream. Here boaters have to take care, when there is a swift flow on the river, as the side weir can be dangerous. Charles Whynne-Hammond, in *Northamptonshire Place Names*, notes that the name of **Wansford** would have originally been 'wielm-ford', meaning 'the ford by the whirlpool'. The village is celebrated for a variety of stories concerning 'Drunken Barnaby' who fell asleep on a haycock, which was swept away on the flooded river. Wansford's ancient bridge, featured in one of these tales, was also the victim of flood water, which damaged it in 1795. The Great North Road once crossed the Nene by this bridge, but now crosses on a 20th-century bridge, high above the water, a short distance downriver. In bygone days, Wansford was a busy inland port. Lighters brought coal and grain upriver and were reloaded with stone from local quarries.

Leaving Wansford, the river turns east and makes a broad sweep around to **Stibbington**, a village between the Nene and the Great North Road. **Sutton** is on the opposite bank. Its church of St Michael and All Angels, dating from 1120, is in a pretty location near to the river. A little further on is Wansford station, which was originally on the Blisworth to Peterborough railway line. The station closed in 1957 and 1972 saw the closure of the railway line. Wansford station is now the headquarters of the preserved Nene Valley Railway, which opened in 1977. Steam trains run from this station to Peterborough, the railway line crossing the Nene on a bridge near Wansford station.

The Nene Valley Railway is almost parallel to the river as far as **Water Newton**, where the lock and former mill are in a delightful setting. Dedicated to St Remigius, Water Newton's Early English church is right on the river bank. A number of Roman antiquities have been dug up in the locality. Between the Nene and **Castor** there were Roman potteries, producing the distinctive 'Castor Ware', while the village of Castor is on the site of a large Roman palace. Below Water Newton, on the south bank of the Nene, is the site of Durobrivae, a Roman town, through which the Roman road, Ermine Street, once ran.

Alwalton is the next settlement downriver. Here, there is a lock and a wooded beauty spot known as Alwalton Lynch. The latter name derives from the Saxon word 'hlinc', meaning bank or ridge. Passing beneath the bridge of the Nene Valley Railway and Milton Ferry Bridge, the river curves past Milton Park on the left-hand bank and Ferry Meadows Country Park, on the opposite side. The latter comprises 500 acres of lakes, woodlands and water meadows and has its own station on the Nene Valley Railway. Just past Bluebell Bridge, a branch from the Nene leads into Overton Lake, where there are overnight moorings for visiting boats. The linear moorings of the Peterborough Yacht Club, with their wooden chalets, are above Orton Lock. This lock, which is electrically operated, is the last before Peterborough is reached. **Orton Longeville**, **Orton Waterville** and **Woodston** are settlements on the south bank of the Nene, while **Longthorpe** is to the north of the river.

The city of **Peterborough** was originally a Saxon settlement known as Medehamstede', meaning 'meadow homestead'. Its present name is derived from that of the great Benedictine abbey of St Peter, which is now Peterborough Cathedral. The abbey was founded in 655 by Peada, the son of King Penda of Mercia. After being laid waste by the Danes in 870, it was restored in 972, but was destroyed by fire in 1116. The building of a new abbey commenced in 1118 and this was consecrated 120 years later in 1238. Katherine of Aragon, the first wife of Henry VIII, was buried here, as was Mary, Queen of Scots, after her execution at Fotheringhay in 1587. The remains of the latter queen were removed to Westminster Abbey in 1612 by her son, James I.

The River Nene once had an important role in the trade of the city and its surrounding agricultural area. In the late 18th century, a good inland trade was carried on with coals, timber, wine and other imports brought upriver from Wisbech to Peterborough, Oundle and Northampton. It was not only goods that were transported by water, but passengers, too. In 1791, two passage boats left Peterborough Quay every Friday morning for Wisbech, returning before noon on Sunday. The coming of the railways took away trade from the river, but, even in the middle of the 19th century, the Nene was still playing its part in the commerce of Peterborough. *Whellan's Directory of Northamptonshire* for 1849, observed that 'The trade of the town is chiefly in corn, coal, timber, and malt, brought in large

5   Houseboats were part of the familiar scene at Peterborough in the early years of the 20th century
and rowing was a favoured form of recreation. Today, this stretch of the river, below Peterborough's
Town Bridge, has been straightened and is known as the Embankment. It now provides pleasant
overnight moorings for boats and good facilities for boat users.

quantities by means of the River Nen and the transit of live and dead stock, and other
agricultural produce to London by railway'.

Until the arrival of the railway, in the mid-1840s, Peterborough was a small place, even
though it had city status on account of its cathedral. However, during the latter part of
the 19th century, there was a rapid rise in its population, as Peterborough became a major
centre for the railways, which spread out in different directions from the city. New
manufacturing industries were developed and brick-making, using the local Oxford clay,
flourished. It was hoped that the improvements made to the river, by the Nene Catchment
Board in the 1930s, would result in Peterborough becoming a thriving inland port. However,
despite the passage upriver of small coastal vessels like the *Constance H* and the *Peterborough
Trader* in 1938, and various other small ships in later years, this expectation was not fulfilled.

A short distance downriver from Peterborough, just past the A1139 road bridge, a
waterway called the King's Dyke branches off to the right. This leads to Stanground Lock,
which gives access to the Middle Level Nene-Ouse navigation link. Leaving the entrance
to King's Dyke, the present course of the River Nene flows through the flat Fenland
countryside in a straight, man-made channel to the electrically operated tidal lock at Dog-
in-a-Doublet, five miles below Peterborough. This cut, which carries on to Guyhirn, was

6 Whittlesey Mere, a very large lake, through which the Old River Nene flowed, was drained in 1851. In the years following the draining of the mere, corn covered the broad expanse of land left, which had once been covered with water. An iron marker, known as the Holme Post, was completely sunk into the peat after the drainage. Over time, this post has been revealed and it measures how much the land has shrunk. By the end of the 20th century the post rose about 13ft. above the ground.

made in 1728 and named Smith's Leam, after Humphrey Smith who supervised the undertaking. Morton's Leam, a cut between Stanground and Guyhirn, constructed by Bishop Morton of Ely in the late 15th century, is to the right. The Nene Washes, rough grassland between the two channels, is used as pasture for cattle during the summer and as a holding ground for winter floods. These washlands are also the habitat of wildfowl and wading birds. After Guyhirn, Bishop Morton continued his leam to Wisbech and the present course of the Nene takes the same route.

From the bridge near Dog-in-a-Doublet Lock, the village of **Thorney** can be reached by turning north. It was once famed for its Benedictine abbey, part of which now forms the parish church. Thorney River, connecting the village with the Nene, was formerly navigable. The market town of **Whittlesey** is to the south of the lock. Dominating the town is the fine, crocketed spire of St Mary's Church, which surmounts a lofty 15th-century tower. Well-known, in the past, for its brickworks, Whittlesey has a number of interesting buildings, many of them constructed of the local brick. Today, Whittlesey is on the Nene-Ouse navigation link, Whittlesey Dyke connecting with the Old River Nene at **Floods Ferry**.

In past times, the course of the Old River Nene took a sharp turn to the south east near Stanground and flowed into a vast, shallow lake called Whittlesey Mere. The mere was one of the places visited during a Fenland pleasure cruise, organised by George Walpole,

3rd Earl of Orford, in the summer of 1774. The earl and his friends used a gang of Fenland lighters for the trip and had a good time with sailing and sporting activities on the mere, where they met up with the Earl of Sandwich, who was First Lord of the Admiralty.

Emerging from this inland sea, which no longer exists, due to draining in Victorian times, the river made for **Ramsey**, once situated on an island in the fens. A branch of the river used to flow through one of Ramsey's streets called the Great Wight. Historically, the town is noted for its abbey, which is said to have been inaccessible except by water. The ruined gatehouse of Ramsey Abbey, now owned by the National Trust, is among the few remains of this rich Benedictine abbey, founded in 969 and dedicated to St Mary and St Benedict.

Nowadays, the Old River Nene winds from near Ramsey, through **Benwick**, to the market town of **March**, notable for its church, dedicated to St Wendreda, which has a striking, double hammer-beam roof decorated with 120 carved angels. During Tudor times, March was a small inland port, but by the mid-19th century it was situated on an important waterway with a considerable trade in coal, corn and timber to places such as Cambridge, Wisbech, King's Lynn, Peterborough, St Ives and Bedford. The town went on to become a railway centre with many of its male inhabitants being engaged in work connected with the railway.

Leaving March, the Old Nene makes for Marmont Priory Lock, where it connects with Well Creek, an eight-mile stretch of canalised river, which runs to Salter's Lode Lock at the end of the Nene-Ouse Navigation Link. Along Well Creek are the villages of **Upwell** and **Outwell**. In Saxon times, they comprised one settlement called Wella. Both Upwell and Outwell were once connected to Wisbech by a tramway, which operated steam trams. Outwell was also linked to the River Nene, at Wisbech, by the long-gone Wisbech Canal.

Downstream of Dog-in-a-Doublet Lock, the River Nene is tidal for 25 miles to the Wash. The waterway flows in a straight line to **Guyhirn**. Worthy of note here is the Puritan Chapel of Ease, which may have been partly built of stone from the ruined Thorney Abbey, though local brick was also used in its construction. **Wisbech**, often dubbed the 'Capital of the Fens', is another seven miles downriver. In medieval times, the town was an important port and centre for trade, being on the Well Stream, the main outfall of the tidal rivers Nene and Ouse. The name of Wisbech is said to have been derived from 'Ouse Beach'. However, after the estuary to the Wash became silted up, the Ouse was diverted to King's Lynn and Wisbech became distanced from the sea. The drainage of the Fens in the 17th century and the construction of a new channel for the Nene to The Wash, completed in 1831, brought prosperity to the town and Wisbech became the centre of a flourishing agricultural area, which was able to transport its produce by water.

The fine architecture of Wisbech bears witness to the growth of the town during the 18th century and first half of the 19th century. One of its gems is the Georgian Peckover House, situated on the outstanding North Brink and owned by the National Trust. The

7   Well Creek, Upwell, *c.*1906. In past times, craft called Fenland lighters traded on the River Nene, the Old River Nene and Well Creek. They were flat-bottomed boats, which were about 42ft. long and 10ft. wide. They carried between 20 and 25 tons of cargo and were linked together in 'gangs'. Horses and, later on, steam tugs were used to pull these lighter trains. The first vessel in this train of Fenland lighters is a 'house lighter', fitted with a cabin. The two men working the gang of lighters would have used it as living quarters. White 'nosings' were painted on the bows of the lighters, so that they would show up in the dark.

Georgian brewery, at the southern end of North Brink, has been in operation for over 200 years. Owned by the Elgood family since 1878, it is renowned for its real ales, which can be sampled by visitors who take a guided tour of the premises. Octavia Hill, co-founder of the National Trust, was born at South Brink, across the river. Both Brinks and the river between them make a very impressive feature of the town. Away from the waterside, there are other buildings of interest. The Castle is a Regency villa, erected by developer Joseph Medworth in 1816, while the Georgian buildings of The Crescent, Ely Place and Union Place form a circus around the Castle. Nearby is the Wisbech and Fenland Museum, founded in 1835, though the building dates from 1847, making it one of the earliest museums to have been built for its purpose.

There are still some 18th- and 19th-century warehouses on both sides of the river, below Town Bridge. In past times, tall sailing ships used to moor at Nene Quay, but the modern fixed Freedom Bridge, a little way downstream, means that it would not be possible for tall craft to do this today. Although trading on the river has declined, Wisbech is making a good effort to accommodate visiting pleasure craft and overnight moorings have been much improved during recent years. Below Freedom Bridge are the quays of the Port of Wisbech, which can handle the cargoes of sea-going ships of up to 2,000 tonnes.

Eight miles downriver is Port Sutton Bridge, where the recently-renovated docks are capable of handling ships of up to 3,500 tonnes. **Sutton Bridge**, in Lincolnshire, is the location of the last bridge over the River Nene. This is the Cross Keys swing bridge, which allows sea-going craft to travel upriver to Wisbech. In the days before a bridge was here, passing over the Cross Key Wash, on the road from Boston to King's Lynn, could be a hazardous experience. A close watch had to be kept on the state of the tides and there were tide tables available, which gave the proper times for negotiating the crossing. However, even in 1830, when the first Cross Keys Bridge was built, the tidal sands at each end of the structure still posed a danger to travellers.

From Sutton Bridge, it is about four miles to Crab's Hole at The Wash, the outfall of the river. The distance the Nene has travelled from Northampton is just over 91 miles and there have been 38 locks along the way. During its journey to the sea, the slow-moving river has winded through verdant water meadows and shady woodland. It has passed by fine old churches, stately

8   In the latter part of the 19th century, shipping was an important trade in the town of Wisbech. Corn, potatoes, bones, wool, seeds, coal, timber and iron were among the imports. The main exports were coal and salt, the latter coming into Wisbech from Worcestershire via the Midland Railway. This postcard view of sailing ships at Wisbech was posted in September 1907, but the photograph may have been taken some years earlier.

homes, stone-built villages, busy towns and a cathedral city, steeped in history. Finally, after flowing in its man-made channel through flat Fenland, it passes between twin white towers, known as the 'lighthouses', before reaching its journey's end.

NORTHAMPTON

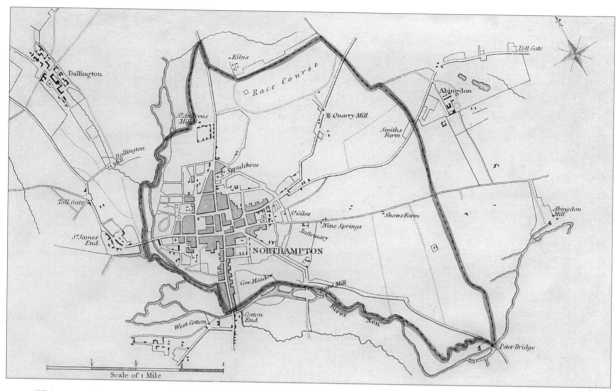

9 This map, dating from *c.*1835, shows the River Nene, on the south side of Northampton, having been joined by its northern branch at Cotton End. The spelling of the River Nene appears as Nen on the map. This corresponds with the way the name of the river is pronounced in the locality. (See caption 60.)

10 South Bridge had been rebuilt and widened a short time before this view, dating from *c.*1912, was taken. Motor transport is conspicuous by its absence. The milk churn on the handcart, at the far end of the bridge, is reminiscent of days when fresh milk was ladled out into customers' own jugs, while the covered wagon adds to the atmosphere of times past. An advertisement, on the side wall of the three-storey building, at the end of the bridge, indicates that the premises were used by 'Matthews implement and wheel works, shoeing and general smith'.

11   Rowing boats were a feature of Northampton's waterside in the early years of the 20th century. South Bridge was the starting point for a voyage down the Nene by skiff, an account of which appears in P. Bonthron's *My holidays on inland waterways* (1916). Peter Bonthron and his friends, having procured a fully-equipped skiff from Collins' boathouse, hoisted the skiff's sail and, on the first day, sailed down to Irthlingborough 'under the most delightful and perfect conditions', the journey taking 11 hours. The boating party had to work the numerous locks themselves and found that they were 'in fair condition, although requiring a deal of handling in some cases, through their comparative disuse'.

12   Northampton Lock and river, *c.*1910. Northampton Lock was formerly called Cow Meadow Lock, as the park through which the Nene flows, after leaving the lock, was once named Cow Meadow. The lock is sometimes referred to as Town Lock. Originally built in 1761, it was reconstructed by the Nene Catchment Board, in the 1930s, when the river was improved. At that time, it was given semi-radial gates, but these were not required after the installation of the sluice at Nunn Mills, further downstream. Nowadays, Northampton Lock is not typical of the present-day Nene locks. It does not have the guillotine gate, at its tail end, which is usually connected with this waterway. Both sets of gates are pointed, as are the gates at the following two locks, Rush Mills Lock and Abington Lock.

13 The bottom gates of Northampton Lock stand open in this view dating from before the start of the First World War. To the left is the weir, while in the background a railway bridge carries the line of the Bedford & Northampton Branch of the Midland Railway over the Nene. This branch line opened in 1872. The passenger service closed in 1962 and the freight service ceased in 1964.

14 Small craft could once be hired at the boathouse adjacent to Northampton Lock. This old postcard view dates from before the First World War, when the boathouse was newly built. In more recent times, the building displayed a mural on its side wall, featuring the Fellows, Morton & Clayton narrowboat, *Northwich*. The boathouse, a well-known venue on the riverside, was destroyed by fire in 1989.

15 This view of the river and promenade dates from *c*.1910. The towpath of the River Nene went through Cow Meadow, which is now known as Becket's Park. It was a popular place for small boys. Chains were looped against the brickwork on the riverside, in case anyone fell into the water. The 18-acre park is named after Thomas à Becket, Archbishop of Canterbury during the reign of Henry II, who was murdered at Canterbury Cathedral in 1170.

16 Thomas à Becket's Well, *c*.1916. Archbishop Becket, once a close personal friend of Henry II, had a succession of charges brought against him by the king. After a trial at Northampton Castle, the archbishop escaped captivity by fleeing. He is said to have stopped for a drink at the well, which now bears his name. The well, rebuilt by the town's corporation in 1843, in the Early English style of architecture, was restored in 1984. It is situated opposite Becket's Park.

17 Another national figure connected with North-ampton was Oliver Cromwell, who is said to have slept in this gabled, town house in Marefair, before the Battle of Naseby in June 1645. Old postcards name the building as Cromwell House, but it is also known as Hazelrigg House, as it is thought to have been built in the early 17th century for the Haselrig or Hazelrigg family. Luckily, the mansion survived the Great Fire of Northampton of 1675 and is one of the town's remaining historic buildings.

18 Most of the medieval building of All Saints' Church was destroyed in the fire of 1675, but the tower and the crypt below the chancel survived. Reconstruction of the church took place between 1676 and 1680. The present building incorporates the 14th-century tower, which is surmounted by a cupola dating from 1704. Another feature of this interesting church is its splendid dome, supported by four great Ionic columns inside. The wide portico, topped by a statue of Charles II in Roman costume and contemporary wig, was added in the early 18th century. The main streets of the town spread out from the focal point of All Saints'.

19 Originally, only the west side of this busy thoroughfare was known as The Drapery, the east side being called The Glovery. As its name suggests, the latter was formerly occupied by people who made gloves. The horse bus, on the right of this view, advertises apparel from Adnitts', a store in the street. This was once operated by brothers Frederick and Charles Adnitt, the business having been acquired in 1874. The building on the right, behind the horse bus, no longer exists. It was once the premises of Norman Goldsmith & Co., wine and spirit merchants, and was demolished to make way for the Westminster Bank, which was opened in 1928.

20 Gold Street takes its name from the Jewish goldsmiths who, centuries ago, were in trade at the eastern end of the street. The entrance to the *Grand Hotel* is on the left of this view, dating from *c.*1910, which looks westwards towards Marefair. A tram is making its way down the street. Northampton's electric tramway system was laid during 1904 and electric trams, resplendent in red and cream, replaced horse trams, which had operated since 1881.

21   The Market Square in Northampton is one of the largest in England. In the mid-19th century, a market for fruit and vegetables was held on Wednesdays here, while one for corn, cattle, sheep, pigs and all sorts of provisions was held on Saturdays, the latter being very well-attended. An impressive drinking fountain, cast by Messrs. Barwell & Co., once stood in this cobbled expanse. It was erected in 1863 to celebrate the marriage of Prince Albert Edward, the future Edward VII, and Princess Alexandra of Denmark. By 1962, the fountain was thought to be in a dangerous state, so it was demolished. The stone base survived for another 10 years before its removal. Markets are still held in the square on several days each week.

HANDSEWERS AT
MANFIELD & SONS'
BOOT FACTORY,
NORTHAMPTON.

22   An old saying holds that, 'you know when you are within a mile of Northampton, by the noise of the cobblers' lapstones'. A variation of this is, 'by the smell of the leather'. The census return of 1841 showed that nearly one in three of the men in the town was a shoemaker. In the 19th century, the army, the colonies, and the principal markets of the United Kingdom were all supplied with boots and shoes from North-ampton. This trade card depicts handsewers at Manfield & Sons, Boot Factory, c.1909.

23 Nunn Mills, *c.*1906. Nunn Mills was downstream of Northampton Lock and on the outskirts of the town. The name was derived from the Cluniac nuns of nearby Delapre Abbey, to which the property once belonged. It was called Nunn Mills, in the plural, as the premises housed three mills under the same roof. In the 1860s, Joseph Westley of Blisworth leased the mills. He used boats on the River Nene to transport wheat to Nunn Mills and to bring coal to power the steam engine he had introduced. In the late 19th century, Joseph's sons joined with A.W. Clark to form the business of Westley Bros. & Clark. Animal feed was manufactured here by Vitovis Ltd. during the last years of the mills' existence. The premises closed in 1968 and Avon Cosmetics went on to redevelop the site.

CLIFFORD HILL

24 Clifford Hill Mill, *c.*1907. According to Domesday Book, there were many mills along the River Nene at the time of the Norman Conquest, a mill at Clifford Hill being among them. In 1914, the mill was operated by both water and steam power. Then, the miller was F.A. Mead. By the 1930s, the corn mill had become disused and was later taken over for gelatine production. Coal, to power the mill, was brought by narrowboat until the 1950s, after which it was delivered by road. The mill was demolished in recent times.

COGENHOE

25   Cogenhoe Mill is one of the 21 mills, which were situated on the River Nene between Northampton and Thrapston. It is three storeys high and built of brick, while the two-storeyed mill house is constructed of stone. In 1890, the water-powered mill was operated by George Valentine and, in 1914, by Thomas Walker. Today, Cogenhoe Mill no longer grinds corn and a caravan site and moorings are adjacent to the property. A short distance uphill from the mill and lock is St Peter's Church, while the village of Cogenhoe is further up the slope.

26   Village street, c.1915. Attractive bands of darker stone, at intervals, on the front of this pair of cottages and the thatched building to the side, make this peaceful corner of Cogenhoe look charming. The tower of St Peter's Church can just be seen behind the roof of another dwelling, further down the lane. Church and census records chart the changes in village trades during the 19th century, when traditional rural occupations were accompanied by those in ironstone mining, the railway and the boot and shoe industry.

27 May Day, or Beltane in the Celtic calendar, marked the beginning of summer and, in past times, was a festival celebrating the fertility of the land. It was once a traditional part of Northamptonshire village life and was among the highlights of the year for children. Garlands would be made with sweet-smelling spring flowers and a May Queen would be chosen and crowned. There were processions and dancing, accompanied by the singing of old May Day folk songs. This maypole scene shows the May Day festivities at Cogenhoe in 1907.

EARLS BARTON

28 Situated on higher ground, above the flood plain, the impressive Saxon tower of the church of All Saints can clearly be seen from the river. Built in the late 10th century, the tower has elaborate decorations in the form of raised vertical strips with long-and-short-work at the angles, which gives an impression of timber work. The battlements are a later addition. The south doorway, with its zigzag decorations, dates from Norman times. To the north of the church is a mound, which once formed the motte of a Norman castle.

LITTLE IRCHESTER

29 Today, a modern road bridge crosses the Nene near Little Irchester. Beyond the bridge is Whitworth's Victoria Mill. Built in 1866, it was substantially enlarged during the 20th century. This mill was the last business regularly to use the upper river for transport. Carrying grain to the mill, by narrowboat, ceased in 1969. Speciality flours are produced at the mill today, which trades under the name of Whitworth Bros. Ltd.

WELLINGBOROUGH

30 In the mid-19th century, Wellingborough's parish church was known as the church of St Luke and All Saints. Early 20th-century postcards labelled it St Luke's, but it is now referred to as All Hallows' Church. The contrasting ironstone and grey stone of the 13th-century tower and the broach spire make for an interesting exterior, while inside, among the notable features, are elaborately carved medieval misericords. The latter are narrow shelf-like secondary seats under the seats of the stalls, against which those taking part in long church services could rest. One of the misericords shows a sedentary workman, balancing a board on his knees upon which are laid tools. He is holding a knife and cutting out a rose shape. In the past, this carving was thought to have been a shoemaker, indicating the importance of shoemaking in the town as far back as the 14th century. However, others maintain that the craftsman depicted on the misericord, is a wood carver, perhaps the very one who fashioned the carvings on the seats.

31 The *Angel Hotel* in Silver Street had been in existence for a long time before this view was taken *c.*1916. The innkeeper in 1830 was Jacob Anthony. In 1849, the proprietor was Mary Leete and the hostelry was then known as the *Angel Commercial Inn*. It was noted in *Kelly's Directory of Northamptonshire* of 1903 that an omnibus from the *Angel Hotel* met trains from the London and North Western railway station. At that time, the proprietor was Benjamin Finch. By 1914, Albert Charles Warwick operated the hotel.

32 Wellingborough's Corn Exchange provided a focal point for this early 20th-century view of the Market Square. Erected in 1861, it was built of red and white brick with Bath stone dressings. The clock tower contained an illuminated clock. Inside, there was a large hall, capable of seating 700, in which were held the corn market, musical entertainments and public meetings. At the time this photograph was taken, it had not yet become the 'Electric Theatre', where audiences could watch short films alternated with variety performances. Later, the building became the Regal Cinema. Visitors seeking a glimpse of the Corn Exchange today would look in vain, as it was demolished in 1959.

33 The *Hind Hotel* dates from at least the 17th century. Oliver Cromwell is said to have stayed at this inn, prior to the Battle of Naseby in 1645. *Pigot & Co.'s Directory* of 1823-4 noted that a coach from the *Hind* left for London every morning, at five in the summer and six in the winter, returning every evening at seven o'clock. In 1914, Wallis John Ford operated the hotel, which was advertised as 'family & commercial & posting house'. At this time, George Octavius Nevett was the landlord of the *Crown*, which is on the extreme left of this view of the Market Square. Next to the inn was the shop of drapers, Green & Valentine.

34 Market Street, *c*.1908. The gabled half-timbered building, on the left, had been recently built, when this street scene was photographed. It housed Boots the Chemists and the Noble and Billingham store. Above the sign for the latter, a board advertises the *Cosy Cafe*. In the middle distance, a sign for the *Old King's Arms* is displayed, the inn itself being just around the bend and out of view. On the extreme right is the shop window of the chemist, John Smith, which has a display of cow horns.

35 Old houses, Sheep Street, *c*.1910. The foundations of these thatched houses date from medieval times or possibly even earlier, though the upper storey was built in the late 16th century. Restoration of the houses took place in 1920. Formerly, Sheep Street was the venue for an annual sheep fair, which was held on 29 October, St Luke's Day.

HIGHAM FERRERS

36   In times past, when roads were poor, wharves such as Higham Wharf were important to the riverside communities. Like other settlements along the river, Higham Ferrers and Rushden, its near neighbour, were involved in the boot- and shoe-making industry. Before the coming of the railways, the Nene was used for the transport of these leather goods. Another local commodity, carried on the river, was bricks. Those made at the brickworks, south of Higham Wharf, were loaded on to boats at the wharf and transported up and downriver. The chimneys of the brickworks can be seen in the background of this view, dating from *c*.1909. The building on the left was the *Anchor Inn*. Past proprietors were John Hawkes in 1823, Elizabeth Hawkes in 1841 and James West from 1847 to 1876. Thomas Middleton was at the *Anchor* in 1903. During the First World War, the *Anchor* ceased to be a public house, but carried on selling refreshments to riverside visitors in the 1920s. It appears that the wharf attracted quite a trade in pleasure boating. Small boats were kept in a shed, open to the river, which had an adjacent landing stage. There was also a swimming area near the boat shed. Higham Wharf and its notoriously low bridge were cut off from the navigation, when the latter was redirected alongside the A45 road.

37 The church of St Mary the Virgin, dating from the 13th century, is a very impressive building. The tower, built between 1250 and 1280, has a close link with the sculpture work at Westminster Abbey. Soaring to 170 feet, the crocketed spire is a landmark in the neighbourhood. It was originally erected in the 14th century, but was replaced in 1631, after it had fallen down. The church has associations with Henry Chichele, Archbishop of Canterbury from 1414 to 1433, who was born in Higham Ferrers. Inside, there are memorial brasses to the archbishop's brother, William, and his wife, Beatrix, and a decorated cross to the archbishop's parents, Thomas and Agnes. Archbishop Chichele's portrait can be seen on the carved misericords, tip-up seats in the stalls. Close by the western end of the church is the former Grammar School, which was built during the 15th century in the Perpendicular style.

38 Bands of ironstone and grey stone are a distinctive feature of the Bede House. It is situated to the south of St Mary's Church across the churchyard, which contains a cross dating from the 14th century. Bede House was founded by Archbishop Chichele, in 1428, and provided living accommodation for 12 elderly men, who were looked after by a Bedeswoman. The Bedesmen each had a screened-off cubicle for sleeping and a cupboard for their possessions. Their allowance was a penny a day and free firing. Although Bedesmen no longer live in the Bede House, the custom of appointing them still continues. Every year, on 21 December, St Thomas's Day, a service is held for them in St Mary's Church, after which a meal is served in the Bede House.

39 College Street is named after Archbishop Chichele's College, founded in the 15th century, the ruins of which can still be seen nearby. Market Square, adjacent to College Street, has the Market Cross as its focal point. This dates from the 14th century, its original, stepped base having been superseded by a conical foundation. Formerly, there were three weekly markets held here on Mondays, Thursdays and Saturdays.

IRTHLINGBOROUGH

40 Irthlingborough, on the left bank of the Nene, is connected to Higham Ferrers by two bridges. The 14th-century stone bridge, shown here, is situated on a sharp bend in the river and can be hazardous to navigate, especially in times of flood. It has ten arches, each of which is shaped differently. Grooves, cut in the parapet by towing ropes, are reminders of the days when craft were hand-hauled through the navigation arch, as there was no towing path through the bridge. The newer, concrete bridge, erected in 1936, upstream of the medieval bridge, carries the A6 high above the water meadows.

41 St Peter's Church, situated between the little town of Irthlingborough and the river, is an impressive sight with its tall ironstone and grey stone tower, which has octagonal storeys. The tower, detached from the church, once belonged to a college of five secular canons and four clerks, ruled by a dean. The latter was originally founded in the 14th century by mercer John Pyel, a Lord Mayor of London. His widow completed the building of the college after his death. The tower was taken down and rebuilt between 1887 and 1893, after having been in a dangerous state for many years. This engraving of the church dates from 1813.

42 The Cross, *c.*1903. According to *Whellan's Directory of Northamptonshire* of 1849, the 13ft. shaft of Irthlingborough's ancient market cross was 'the standard for adjusting the provincial pole, by which the doles or portions in the meadows are measured'. This referred to the days when strip farming was practised. The Cross, with its graduated, stepped base, is adorned with two gas lamps in this view, which looks up Finedon Road. It was moved from this site to its present position, a short distance to the south, during the mid-1960s.

STANWICK

43 Stanwick is situated on high ground, overlooking the valley of the Nene. Dating from the 13th century, St Lawrence's Church has a striking octagonal tower, crowned by a spire rising to about 156ft. Among the rectors of the church were the fathers of John Dolben, a 17th-century Archbishop of York, and Richard Cumberland, an 18th-century playwright. The name of Stanwick's public house, the *Duke of Wellington*, commemorates the victor of the Battle of Waterloo. His famous boots are said to have been made in the village.

LITTLE ADDINGTON

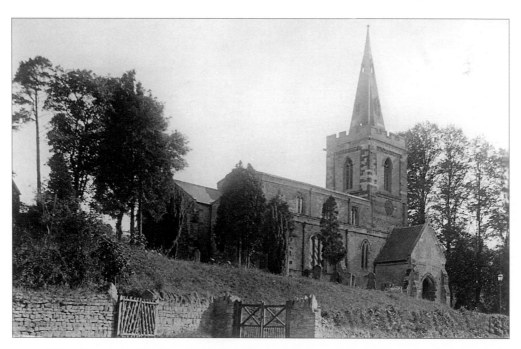

44 When Domesday Book was compiled, there was only a single settlement in this locality. It was called Edintone, meaning the 'farmstead where Eadda's people lived'. In time, when the population expanded, two communities developed, Great Addington being the mother village and Little Addington becoming the daughter village. Situated on high ground to the west of the Nene, the church of St Mary at Little Addington has a mid-14th-century embattled tower with a short spire. The church overlooks a picturesque village of stone and thatch.

GREAT ADDINGTON

45 Great Addington's church is in the background of this early 20th-century postcard view. Dedicated to All Saints, it has a monument inside to Sir Henry de Vere who died in 1516. The inn, on the right, advertising Praed's Fine Ales & Porter, is the *Hare & Hounds*. Past proprietors were Thomas Chapman in 1849 and George Knight in 1903. By 1914, David Payne was the innkeeper. The covered delivery cart belonging to Weekley of Ringstead and the coal cart, outside the hostelry, contribute to the interesting scene. In 1903, the carrier, Lot Weekley, passed through Great Addington to Wellingborough each Wednesday.

WOODFORD

46 The church of St Mary the Virgin is in a delightful position, overlooking the River Nene. Its earliest parts date from Norman times, while the tower was begun in the 13th century and the spire was added in the 14th century. One of its claims to fame is the human heart, found wrapped in a cloth in the underside of an interior arch. This was discovered during the restoration work of 1866. The heart may have belonged to Roger de Kirketon, whose body was buried in Norfolk in 1280. He had married a daughter of Robert Maufe, a lord of the manor. After her father's death, she was one of four co-heiresses to the Woodford estate. A more recent revelation was a photograph, taken in the 1960s, showing the ghostly form of a kneeling knight at the altar. This postcard view of the church dates from *c.*1906.

47 The Green, *c.*1910. In past times, the village green at Woodford would be thronged with large crowds enjoying the Feast, held in the second week of July. No doubt the *Duke's Arms*, shown here on the Green, did good trade on these occasions. In 1903, the proprietor was Francis Albert White, while in 1914 Walter Pendred ran the establishment. Previous landlords of the public house were George Fisher in 1851 and Charles Gibson in 1871.

48 This Edwardian postcard, showing boating on the river near the church of St Mary the Virgin, was sent by a visitor staying at Woodford Mill, where accommodation for paying guests was provided. Rowing boats were hired out at the mill where teas were served.

49 Woodford Bottom Mill, also known as Allen's Mill, was built around the middle of the 18th century. According to Eric and Mary Humphries, in *Woodford Juxta Thrapston* (1985), the mill was worked by members of the Hill family in the late 18th and first half of the 19th centuries. Among the first tenants was Samuel Hill, who was succeeded by his sons, Joseph and John. In 1851, Henry Hill was the miller, while William Porter Hill worked the mill in 1861. By 1863, Samuel Allen had taken over the premises. Visitors to the riverside now would look in vain for the mill, as it was demolished some years ago.

50 This photograph of Woodford Lock shows the lock gates with conventional balance beams. It was taken before the improvements to the Nene locks were made in the 1930s by the Nene Catchment Board, under its chairman, George Dallas. Like most other locks on the river, the present Woodford Lock has a vertical steel guillotine gate at the lower end and steel mitred gates at the upstream end. The latter are often referred to as 'pointing doors'. Besides improving the navigation, the locks constructed by the Nene Catchment Board in the 1930s helped with flood prevention. In times of raised water levels, the pointing doors of some of them are chained back and the guillotine gates are lifted to allow flood water to pass through them.

DENFORD

51 Before the creation of Wicksteed Park in Kettering, the River Nene at Denford was a great venue for boating and fishing. There were two boathouses, which catered for folk coming from the neighbouring areas for days out and holidays. One of the boathouses had a large floating landing stage. On one occasion, so many people were stepping in and out of the boats that the landing stage tipped over and everyone fell in the river. The boathouse near Denford Church can be seen in this view of the river, dating from c.1915.

52 This postcard, dating from *c*.1913, shows the charming riverside setting at Denford. Holy Trinity Church, built in the Early English style, is situated close by the River Nene. The 13th-century pinnacled tower has a broach spire with small windows, called lucarnes, set into it.

53 Flooding used to be a frequent occurrence in the Nene Valley. In past times, skating would take place on the frozen, flooded meadows at Denford. It is said that, one year, when the ice on the river was very thick, it was possible to skate from Northampton to Peterborough along the frozen Nene. In *Down the River*, H.E. Bates included boyhood reminiscences of skating in the Nene valley, mentioning that, when the great expanses of flood waters froze, the whole neighbourhood behaved 'with something of the excitement of small children'.

THRAPSTON

54 A view looking towards Islip and Thrapston Bridge, taken from the Midland Road railway station in the early years of the 20th century. Thrapston Mill, with its tall chimney, can be seen in the centre of the picture, next to the railway line. The railway bridge over the Nene, shown here, was later replaced by a brick viaduct with 14 arches. The Midland Road station, opened in 1866, was Thrapston's second railway station. The first was Thrapston Bridge Street station, one of the principal stations on the Nene Valley Line. Both stations closed within a short time of each other: the Midland Road station was closed to passengers on 15 June 1959 and to goods on 28 October 1963, while the Bridge Street station was closed to passengers on 4 May 1964 and to goods on 7 June 1965.

55 At Thrapston, there used to be a large stone corn mill with three storeys, but only its tall brick-built chimney remains today. In 1903, Richard Lines Ridgway was the miller here, while in 1914 John Barrick operated the water mill. The riverside area surrounding the former mill is now known as the Mill Marina. This has moorings for boats and pitches for caravans and tents.

56 This old picture postcard of Midland Road, dating from *c.*1905, recalls the time when horse-drawn traffic was the norm and no cars were in sight. The unusual first-storey window, displaying ladies' wear from Freeman and Webb's drapery shop below, is eye catching.

57 High Street, *c.*1914. A motor cycle stands outside Heighton's Motor Garage, on the left of this view, while next door is the entrance to the former Corn Exchange. The latter, established in 1848, could accommodate 400 people and was also used for public entertainment. Over the doorway, flanked by Tuscan columns, is a wooden plough and carved limestone wheatsheaf. The *King's Arms* is further up the street on the same side. In 1914, William Beal was the landlord.

58 The distinctive figure of a hart once stood above the archway to the yard of the *White Hart Hotel*. A gas lamp, below the figure, lit up the entrance. In 1903, the proprietor of the hotel was William Gilbert Bone, who was also an 'agent by appointment to the London & North Western Railway'. Since this Edwardian view of the very narrow Bridge Street was taken, the buildings on the right-hand side have been demolished and the road has been widened.

59 A busy scene in Bridge Street, probably photographed on a Tuesday market day before the First World War. In the background is the *Swan Hotel*, the opening between the two pillars being the entrance to its yard. The *Swan* was listed in *Pigot & Co.'s Directory* of 1823-4. It was one of six taverns and public houses in Thrapston, its proprietor at that time being William Smith. By 1849, when there were eight hostelries in the town, William Smith was still the innkeeper. Mrs. Anne Farrington was in charge of the premises in 1877 and William Wilson ran the hotel in 1890, when it was known as the *Swan Commercial Hotel & Posting House*. In 1903, George Roberts was the proprietor and there was a horse-drawn conveyance from Bridge Street railway station for patrons of the hotel. Mrs Eliza Morley ran the establishment in 1914.

60 Thrapston Bridge, *c*.1914. A nine-arched medieval bridge, with cutwaters, links the market town of Thrapston with the neighbouring village of Islip. Five of the arches had to be rebuilt after the great flood of 1795 and the narrow packhorse bridge has been widened and altered since it was first erected. At one time, there was a toll to cross the bridge, though soldiers and people going to church were exempt. Bill Warren, in *Thrapston A Glimpse Into The Past* (1987), noted that the toll charges were 2d. for a wagon, three farthings for a horse and 4d. per 20 sheep or 20 cattle. It is round about here that the pronunciation of the word Nene changes. From the source of the river to Thrapston local folk call it the 'Nenn'. However, downstream of Islip, the waterway becomes the 'Neen'.

ISLIP

61 The church of St Nicholas, standing in an elevated position on the west bank of the river, was built in the Perpendicular style and has a pinnacled tower topped by an elegant crocketed spire. The interior is noted for a monument to Mary Washington, the wife of the great-great-great-uncle of George Washington, the first American president. Another interesting feature is the replica brass on the floor of the chancel. This commemorates John Nichol, who was buried here in 1467, and his wife Annys. Their American descendants had the memorial placed here in 1910. Visitors to the church today would look in vain for the lych gate in the position shown here. In 1926, it was moved to Main Street, when the churchyard was enlarged.

62 Islip Mill is situated a short distance downstream of Thrapston Bridge. A map of the river, dating from *c.*1754, shows that a mill was here then. In the late 18th century there were two waterwheels. The two-storeyed mill was converted to electricity in the middle of the 20th century. The last miller was Mr. W.P. Stafford, who, from 1926 to 1960, recorded local and world-wide events on the wooden elevator shaft. A facsimile of some of these records is included in *Islip Past Present And Future* (1995), published by Islip Parish Council. Corn was ground at the mill until 22 August 1960, but the building is now a private residence.

63 The Islip blast furnaces, pictured here in the early years of the 20th century, were about a mile away from Islip along the Thrapston to Kettering Road, the Islip Iron Company having been formed by Charles Plevins in 1871. In its heyday, many men in the area were employed by the company. The tall furnace chimney, belching out smoke, was a landmark in the neighbourhood. Today, it no longer exists and the huge furnaces are no more.

TITCHMARSH

64 A brick-built Methodist chapel is on the left of this view of Chapel Street, but the focal point of the grey stone village of Titchmarsh is its impressive pinnacled Perpendicular church tower, which is in the background. The church of St Mary the Virgin has associations with Mrs Elizabeth Creed (née Pickering), a relative and friend of John Dryden. The poet spent his boyhood at Titchmarsh, where his mother's family, the Pickerings, lived.

65 Titchmarsh Mill and Lock, 1999. In the past, corn was ground at this stone-built water mill, which had six pairs of stones. The last working miller was Alfred Turner, who worked the mill from *c.*1914 to its closure in the 1950s. The mill has been the headquarters of the Middle Nene Cruising Club for the past three decades. Titchmarsh Lock is adjacent to the mill. This photograph shows the guillotine gate raised. Locks on the Nene have to be left like this, in case of heavy rain, as they play an important part in flood control. Titchmarsh Lock is one of the Nene locks which is 'reversed' in times of flood. Then, its pointing doors are chained back to allow flood water to discharge.

ALDWINCLE

66   The village of Aldwincle is distinguished in its possession of two fine churches. All Saints' Church, at one end of the village, is now redundant. A tablet in the church is a memorial to the poet and playwright, John Dryden, who was Poet Laureate between 1670 and 1688. The Old Rectory, opposite All Saints' Church, was the birthplace, in 1631, of the poet. He was the son of Erasmus Dryden of Titchmarsh and his mother was the daughter of the Rev. Henry Pickering, rector of All Saints'. This old postcard view of 'Dryden's House' dates from *c.*1904.

67   St Peter's Church and village school, *c.*1914. The parish church of St Peter dates from the 12th century and is said to have one of the best broach spires in Northamptonshire. Its interior is noted for two stained-glass figures of St Christopher and St George. Carvings of the Green Man, with mouth foliage, are also to be found here. In times past, the latter was a symbol of Nature's fertility. A National School for 100 children was erected in 1872, by subscription. The school was partly maintained by an endowment received from land. In 1890, the endowment was £16 16s. At this time, William Ward was the school master and Miss Lydia Mayes was the assistant school mistress.

WADENHOE

68 Formerly known as the church of St Giles, the church of St Michael and All Angels stands in a prominent position on high ground, overlooking the river and water meadows of the Nene Valley. Its late Norman tower is crowned by an unusual 'saddleback' roof. The six bells in the tower, ranging in date from 1603 to 1937, are rung regularly and are reputed to make the most delightful peal in the locality. A number of graves in the churchyard commemorate the Ward Hunt family who once lived in Wadenhoe House, a substantial mansion overlooking the River Nene.

69 The Rt. Hon. George Ward Hunt of Wadenhoe House was made Chancellor of the Exchequer in 1868 and, in 1874, he became First Lord of the Admiralty. As he needed to keep abreast of the business of the Government, a postal telegraph office was established in Wadenhoe, which was the first in a rural area. The original sign is still on the wall of Wadenhoe's Post Office.

70   A circular limestone dovecot, with a roof of Collyweston tiles, can be found in the village near the beginning of the road to Pilton. Thought to date from between 1793 and 1822, it may be entered through a very low doorway. The ladder, fixed to a framework attached to a central pivoted post, is still in place. Although dovecots usually housed birds for eating, it is feasible that Wadenhoe's dovecot may have provided birds for the pastime of shooting.

71   According to Julia Moss, one of the contributors to *The Story Of Wadenhoe* (1998), Joseph Allen was the tenant of a water mill at Wadenhoe in 1795. His son, John Allen, rented it in 1822, by which time a house was recorded as being on the site. Besides being involved in milling, the Allen family were farmers and, no doubt, they were the employers of folk in the neighbourhood. Francis Allen succeeded his father, John, as miller. At the time of the 1881 census, he was recorded as being 62 years old. His corn-milling business looks as if it was flourishing, judging by the four millers resident in the village, who were presumably his employees. However, after his death in the late 1880s, Wadenhoe Mill suffered a downturn. No millers were recorded in the village in the 1891 census and it was not until 1927 that the mill began to work again. Nowadays, Wadenhoe Mill is a private residence, having been converted in 1972.

ACHURCH

72   Northamptonshire is often referred to as the county of 'squires and spires', because of its many country houses inhabited by local landowners, and for the striking church spires dotting its landscape. It was traditionally held that 32 churches could be seen from high ground near Thrapston. The broach spire of the church of St John the Baptist at Achurch adds to the delightful views along the river between Wadenhoe and Lilford. Access to the churchyard is through the intricately carved oak lych gate, pictured here c.1905, which was designed by the wife of the 4th Baron Lilford, after his death in 1896. A roofed lych gate, such as this, is used as a resting place for coffins before burial.

LILFORD

73 Lilford Hall, *c.*1917. The River Nene flows past the sloping grounds of Lilford Hall, where, in springtime, thousands of daffodils are a delight to the eye. This fine mansion dates from *c.*1635. In 1711, it passed into the ownership of the Powys family. During the second half of the 19th century, a member of the family, the 4th Baron Lilford, created the renowned Lilford aviaries in the grounds. This Lord Lilford also established the little owl in Britain, by releasing into the wild a number of the species, brought from Europe.

74 Lynch Bridges, *c.*1907. Near Pilton, the Nene divides in two and flows through beautiful woodlands, known as the Lynches or Linches, which are managed by the Forestry Commission. The bridge, shown here, crosses the backwater, while Lilford Bridge, in the background, crosses the navigable channel.

PILTON

75   Manor House and church, *c.*1912. Pilton's manor house stands near the parish church and overlooks the meadows sloping down to the River Nene. It was formerly the home of a branch of the Tresham family and here the last of the family lived and died. After the acquisition of the manor, by Sir Thomas Powys of Lilford, it became Pilton's rectory. According to Nikolaus Pevsner, the earliest part of the manor house dates from the 1560s. There was an addition to the building *c.*1620 and in the 1840s the house was altered and improved. The church of St Mary and All Saints, though it has a Norman doorway, dates mainly from the 13th century. Its chancel was rebuilt between 1862 and 1864. The marriage of Erasmus Dryden and Mary Pickering, the parents of the poet, John Dryden, took place in Pilton Church on 21 October 1630.

BARNWELL

76   Barnwell is some way from the Nene, on the further side of the Thrapston to Oundle Road. It originally comprised two separate parishes, known as Barnwell St Andrew and Barnwell All Saints. The name, 'Bairn well' or 'Bernes well', is said to derive from the numerous wells and springs in the locality, which, in the past, were renowned for the cure of children's diseases, though this has been disputed in recent times. According to *Whellan's Directory of Northamptonshire* of 1849, 'The village of Barnwell consists of one long street of straggling houses. A brook runs through the centre, and is crossed by rustic bridges, the side road is planted with elm trees, and forms a pretty rural picture'. The *Montagu Arms*, the building on the left of this village scene, was named after the Montagu family, former owners of the manor and castle at Barnwell. In 1881, the licensed victualler at this inn was John Quincey, while in 1903 the proprietor was F. Quincey.

77 This view, looking across Barnwell Brook to St Andrew's Church, dates from *c.*1914. The 13th-century church is noted for its medieval 'Jack-in-the-Green', a face with sticking-out tongue, which is among the carvings of flowers and leaves on the north doorway. May Day was the festival of the Green Man and, in past times, young men would disguise themselves with a covering of leaves before making eyes at the local girls.

78 A footpath leads from the church to gabled Barnwell Manor, which, until recently, was the home of the Duke and Duchess of Gloucester. The ruins of the 13th-century Barnwell Castle, with its round corner towers, stand in the grounds of the manor house. They are reputed to be haunted by a monk wielding a whip. Strangely enough, the crest of the Le Moine family, who originally occupied the castle, includes a monk and a whip.

79 Two narrowboats waiting to rise in Upper Barnwell Lock, 1999. The present-day locks, with their steel pointing doors at the top end and vertical gates at the bottom end, are of a standard size, 83 ft. 6 in. (25.5 m) long and 15 ft. (4.6 m) wide.

80 Barnwell Mill is adjacent to Upper Barnwell Lock. There has been a mill on the site since Saxon times. The present three-storeyed mill building dates from the 17th century. It is built of local limestone and has a roof made of Collyweston slates. In 1841, John Baker was corn miller here. At the time of the 1881 census, George F. Baker was residing at the Mill House with his five children, mother and six servants. He was described, on the census, as a farmer of 350 acres employing 11 men, four boys and one miller. This view of the flour mill dates from the first decade of the 20th century. Mrs. Frances Baker was miller here in 1914. Barnwell Mill was converted into a restaurant in 1969.

ASHTON

81 There were two mills at Ashton at the time of the Domesday survey, the annual rent for them being £2 and 325 eels. In medieval times and until the Dissolution of the Monasteries, the mills were owned by Peterborough Abbey. Ashton Mill ground corn up to the end of the 19th century. During that century, millers at Ashton included Thomas Compton, 1830, Robert Compton, 1850, John Compton, 1854, Henry Hill, 1877 and William Henry Pollard, 1894. In 1900, the 1st Lord Rothschild converted the mill to generate electricity for the main buildings of the estate at Ashton. Pumping works at the mill supplied the village of Ashton with water from the Nene. The mill machinery ceased to operate around the middle of the 20th century, after dredging of the Nene took away the mill's main source of power. Ashton Mill is now home to the National Dragonfly BioMuseum. A variety of dragonflies and damselflies can be seen during late spring and summer in their habitats around the mill pond and mill race.

OUNDLE

82 The Courthouse is the building on the right of this early 20th-century view of Mill Road, which leads from Barnwell Mill into Oundle. In early Victorian times, the municipal government of the town was chiefly vested in the magistrates for the district, who held petty sessions in the Town Hall. Later, the Courthouse was used. It now houses 'The New Oundle Museum'. Here, the magistrates' room has a display area including an exhibit concerning brewing, an industry important to the town in the past. Agricultural implements are in the courtyard and the museum also has the recreation of a Victorian shop.

83 This view of Oundle's West Street dates from *c.*1905. In the foreground, horse collars hang outside the shop belonging to the saddler and harness maker, Alfred Loveday. The name of Loveday is associated with generations of a family from Islip, who harvested rushes from the Nene for the manufacture of horse collars, baskets, mats and chair seats. Three bundles of rushes were plaited together to make a horse collar and around 50 rushes were needed for the process. The horse collars, like the other rush products of Loveday's factory in Islip, were made entirely by hand.

84 *Talbot Hotel*, New Street, c.1910. The grey stone *Talbot*, with its handsome bay windows, is one of Oundle's finest buildings. Dating from 1626, it is thought to stand on the site of an earlier inn. Its splendid oak staircase is reputed to have come from nearby Fotheringhay Castle. It is said to be the one down which Mary, Queen of Scots walked to her execution in 1587, though some doubt has been cast upon this story. There is a tale that her ghost haunts the stairs and two of the hotel's bedrooms. The *Talbot* was formerly a coaching inn. In 1823, a coach called 'The Regulator' left the *Talbot* for London every Monday, Thursday and Saturday morning at six o'clock. At the time this view was taken, William A. Carley was the proprietor. In Oundle's town guide for 1910, he advertised 'Excellent Accommodation for Hunting Gentlemen, Cyclists and Tourists' plus 'Cuisine & Wines of the Best'. Hacks and hunters were for hire, while motor cars could be accommodated and petrol supplied.

85 Oundle School is the town's famous public school. It was endowed in the 16th century by the will of Sir William Laxton, who became a grocer and Lord Mayor of London. A renowned headmaster of Oundle School was F.W. Sanderson, who led the school for 30 years from 1892 to 1922. It was during this time that a number of the school's buildings were built, including the Great Hall shown in this view, dating from just before the First World War. The wings to the Great Hall had been added in 1910. Further building is taking place in the background.

86 In 1826, stone from the partly demolished All Saints' Church in Barnwell was used in the construction of the old Town Hall in Oundle's Market Place. This building was once used as a literary institute and for public meetings, while the lower part served as a butter market. In the mid-19th century, there was a market on Thursdays and an open-air market is still held here on the same day. In this view of the Market Place, dating from the early 20th century, the shop of fancy draper, F.G. Davidson, is on the left, while that of tailors, Wilkins & Co., is on the right.

87 St Osyth's Lane, *c*.1917. The premises of the *Anchor Inn*, in the foreground of this street scene, are no longer a hostelry. A stone, dated 1637, is on the south gable, but some parts of the property are likely to be older than this date. Now, the low-windowed building is called 'Anchor Inn Cottage', but the adjacent properties no longer exist.

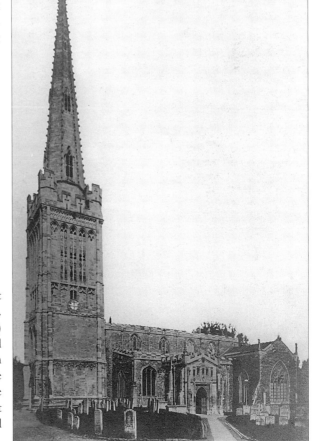

88 The tall crocketed needle spire, topping the elegant tower of St Peter's Church, is a landmark for miles around. Mention is made in Tony Ireson's *Northamptonshire* (1964) of an Oundle schoolboy called Bailey, who, in 1888, climbed the crockets to the top of the spire. Iris Wedgwood, in *Fenland Rivers* (1936), related a similar story, though gave no name for the culprit or date for the feat. However, she noted that, after sound punishment had been meted out by the headmaster, who was ready with his cane, a pound was given to the boy in recognition of his courage.

89 In North Street, opposite the church, stands a gabled bay-windowed building, which was formerly the *White Lion Inn*. The striking bays are said to have been added to an older property in 1641. Past innkeepers include J. Willmott, in 1823, John Hunt, in 1830, Abigail Hunt, in 1841, John Prentice, in 1849, Henry Garner, in 1877, and Harry Palmer in 1903. George Plowright was the proprietor in 1914. A lamp above the door shows the inn's position in this view, dating from *c.*1913 and looking towards the Market Place.

90 North Bridge, *c.*1918. When North Bridge was undergoing repairs in the early 19th century, an inscribed stone was found, which gave information about the rebuilding of the bridge more than two centuries before. The inscription reads, 'IN THE YERE OF OVRE LORD 1570 THES ARCHES WER BORNE DOVNE BY THE WATERS EXTREMYTIE. IN THE YERE OF OVRE LORD 1571 THEY WER BVLDED AGAYN WITH LYME AND STONNE. THANKS BE TO GOD'.

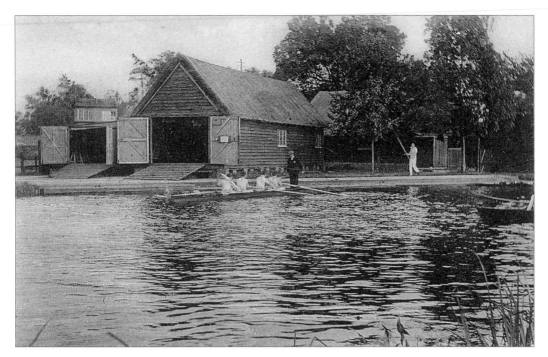

91 Oundle School boathouse at the eastern end of North Bridge, *c.*1900s. In 1916, P. Bonthron, in *My holidays on inland waterways*, observed that 'Pleasure boating is not much indulged in up this way … but we were pleased to note that the Oundle school boys had their rowing club and boathouse. So far as we could trace, there are only a few motor boats on this river, one being a covered lifeboat, made into a houseboat with a stern wheel arrangement. The weeds do not encourage the pastime.'

92 Boating downstream of North Bridge, *c.*1907. Old picture postcards show that there were some sailing craft used for pleasure boating, in the vicinity, during Edwardian times. If one wanted peace and quiet on the river, this locality appears to have been ideal. The message on the back of this old postcard reads, 'This is a lonely spot, no village with more than six houses for miles'.

COTTERSTOCK

93 There was once a tall mill at Cotterstock, which was working well into the second half of the 20th century. 'BB', in *A Summer on the Nene*, mentioned that Cotterstock Mill was 'humming with life', when he cruised the Nene in the mid-1960s, and remarked, 'different indeed to other mills which we were to see on our journey downriver'. Much of the 19th-century mill was destroyed by fire in 1968, but part of it was rebuilt in 1972 and is now a residence. James Rickett was miller at Cotterstock in 1830, while John Everest, senior, ran the water mill in 1841. By 1881, the Smith family were corn millers at Cotterstock. Groome and Richardson were millers here in 1903. In 1914, Siddons & Sons operated the mill. This view of Cotterstock Mill was posted on 26 May 1917 by a visitor staying with Mrs Slater at the *Gate Inn*.

94 The tall chancel of Cotterstock's church of St Andrew faces the Nene. Its erection, in *c.*1337-8, was connected with the establishment of a chantry or college here by John Gifford, a former rector of the parish and a canon at York. The college was founded for a provost, 12 chaplains and two clerks to pray for the royal family, the founder and benefactors and for their souls when they died. It was dissolved in the 16th century. This 1999 riverside view of the ancient church, with its square embattled tower, has probably not changed very much over the last 100 years.

95 Cotterstock Hall was possibly built in Jacobean times, though the date on the central gable is 1658, when the house was altered by John Norton. The poet, John Dryden, spent the last two summers of his life at Cotterstock Hall and it was here that he wrote his *Fables*, while staying with Elizabeth Steward, the daughter of his relative and friend, Mrs Elizabeth Creed.

TANSOR

96 This view of boating on the river near St Mary's Church, in the early years of the 20th century, shows a tranquil scene. However, the church is so close to the Nene that sometimes flood water comes up to the churchyard. Early parts of the building date from Norman times. Inside, points of interest are the seven stalls, which were brought from the collegiate church of Fotheringhay. They have misericords, which feature carvings of a falcon and fetterlock, the badge of the House of York.

97 Children pose for the photographer in this old postcard view, dating from *c.*1916 and showing the village Post Office and St Mary's Church. In past times, one of Tansor's two bakehouses was at the back of the Post Office. Thomas Sawford, baker, was also victualler at the *White Horse* in the mid-19th century. Tansor once had another public house, the *Black Horse*, but both of these hostelries, like the former Post Office, are now private residences.

98 Village street, *c.*1916. In the days before motor traffic, children played freely in the street. The boys to the left of this group of children are holding hoops, one big and one small. Hoops, sometimes known as 'bowlers' in Northamptonshire, could be made of iron or of wood. A short stick was used to bowl them along. Other street games included 'whip and top', hopscotch, skipping and marbles.

PERIO MILL

99   The Bradshaw family occupied Perio Mill in 1881. Head of the household was Benjamin Bradshaw, miller and grazier. In the 1881 census, his age was recorded as 69, while his wife Elizabeth was 53 years old. Two unmarried sons, aged 28 and 23, also lived at the mill. The household included 16-year-old John Martin, a domestic servant. In 1914, Ebenezer Bradshaw was miller here. This photograph of Perio Mill, taken in 1999, shows a low building, which is in sharp contrast to the other taller mills along the riverside.

FOTHERINGHAY

100   The magnificent church of St Mary and All Saints, at Fotheringhay, is situated in a prime position on the banks of the Nene, its octagonal lantern a landmark for some distance around. It was once a collegiate church, with a close link to the House of York. The quire of the college, in the eastern part of the building, formed a separate church from the nave in the western part, which was the parish church. The college buildings and the quire were dismantled in 1548 by John Dudley, Duke of Northumberland.

101　There was once a wooden bridge across the River Nene at Fotheringhay. After Elizabeth I stayed here during one of her progresses, she gave the order that a new bridge should be built. An inscribed tablet on the bridge commemorated its erection in 1573. When this structure in stone and timber fell into decay, the present humped-backed bridge was built in 1722. Stone from a quarry at nearby King's Cliffe was used in its construction. This view, dating from *c*.1914, shows that the four arches are at different heights. The low central navigation arch can pose difficulties for boaters negotiating the bridge.

102　A grass-covered mound and a lump of masonry beside the Nene are among the remains of Fotheringhay Castle, famous as the place where Mary, Queen of Scots was put on trial and executed in 1587. Legend has it that the Scottish thistles growing on the mound, among the hawthorn bushes, were planted during her captivity at the castle. They are sometimes referred to as 'Queen Mary's Tears'.

103 Inns in the village's main street catered for visitors who could not be accommodated at Fotheringhay Castle. This early 20th-century view shows the former *New Inn*, more recently known as Garden Farm. The stone building may have been erected by Edward IV, as the large arch over the entrance gateway bears the arms of the house of York. It was here that the executioner of Mary, Queen of Scots is said to have stayed. A survey, taken in 1624, indicated that the main part of the *New Inn* contained 'a hall, a parlour, a kitchen and diverse other chambers'. The row of cottages, opposite Garden Farm, once comprised the *Old Inn*, thought also to have been built during the reign of Edward IV.

WARMINGTON

104 Dedicated to St Mary the Virgin, the church at Warmington was built between 1180 and 1280. It is notable for its striking broach spire with three tiers of small projecting windows. The village was a farming community in the late 19th century and the chief crops grown in the locality were hay, barley and wheat. In 1890, among the farmers in the neighbourhood were Robert Godfrey of Warmington Grange, James Heys of the Lodge, Edward Stokes of Manor Farm and Thomas Stokes of Home Farm.

ELTON

105   Elton Mill, *c.*1914. In 1881, Elton Mill appears to have been flourishing, as the miller, Henry S. Smith, a farmer of 233 acres, employed four men and a boy at the mill. When the author and illustrator 'BB' wrote *A Summer on the Nene* in 1967, he recalled that the previous year Elton Mill had appeared to be derelict. However, he heard from someone in the village that the mill still ground beans and corn for the estate using electricity rather than water power.

106   Elton Hall has been home to the Proby family for over 350 years. Sir Thomas Proby undertook the rebuilding of a house on the site in the 1660s, and this structure was altered and enlarged during the 18th and 19th centuries. This view of the Hall dates from *c.*1912. The library is renowned for its fine books including Henry VIII's prayer book, which contains the handwriting of the monarch and two of his six wives.

NASSINGTON

107 The church of St Mary and All Saints, *c.*1911. The octagonal belfry stage on the tower of Nassington Church is topped by a crocketed spire, which dates from 1640. Remains of the stonework of a Saxon church are to be found in the interior, along with part of the shaft of a Saxon cross, depicting the Crucifixion. Other features of antiquity, within the church, include the remnants of medieval wall paintings. These were brought to light during the 1880s by the Rev. Daniel Barrett, who used a small penknife to detach the limewash covering them. St Mary and All Saints' has a 'conservation churchyard', which is looked upon as an important sanctuary for wildlife. A survey has identified 40 different wild flowers growing in the churchyard, among a variety of trees and shrubs. The location is also the haunt of a number of different types of birds and butterflies.

108 The Prebendal Manor House, opposite Nassington Church, is said to be among England's oldest continually occupied houses. It was erected in the 13th century, on the site of a late Saxon manor, as the residence for a prebendary of Lincoln Cathedral. The prebendary was a canon who ran the estate for the Bishop of Lincoln, the owner of the land. Part of the outside of the Great Hall is shown here. This was where people, who worked for the prebendary, ate and slept. It was also used to entertain the guests of the prebendary and for courts of law, which were possibly held on several occasions each year. Today, the Prebendal Manor House and its recreated medieval garden are open to visitors.

109   Behind the peaceful facade of Nassington village in this old postcard view, dating from *c*.1913, a number of tradespeople were in business. In 1914, there were two grocers, Walter S. Dixon and M.H. Mould, and two bakers, Elijah Dixon and Albert Chambers. The butcher was George Mould. Miss E. Watson ran the laundry, while George Spriggs dealt with repairs to boots and shoes. There were four public houses in the village at this time. The *Black Horse*, originally built *c*.1674, was operated by Mrs. Frances Morris and Joseph Thomas Scotney was in charge of the *Queen's Head*. The proprietor of the *Three Horse Shoes* was E.J. Knight, while that of the *Three Mill Bills* was William Scotney.

YARWELL

110   The church of St Mary Magdalene at Yarwell dates from the 13th century. It was altered in the late 18th century, the aisles being taken down. The tower has a pyramidal roof and contains a 13th-century window. A feature of the interior is the tomb of Humphrey Bellamy, dated 1715. There is a local tradition that Humphrey stopped in Yarwell, on his way to London, when he was a penniless lad. He was ill, so kind-hearted villagers looked after him until he went on his way again. Their generosity was not forgotten. Later in life, Humphrey became a London merchant. After his death, money was left to buy bread for the poor, which was to be laid on his tombstone on 21 December, St Thomas's Day.

111   Yarwell Mill, erected in 1839, is a large stone building of three storeys. The adjoining mill house may have been built earlier. In 1881, Henry Jelley was the miller here. He was also a farmer of 500 acres, employing 16 men and nine boys. George Robinson operated the mill in 1914. Today, Yarwell Mill, like so many other mills along the Nene, is no longer working.

112 This view of Yarwell Lock, dating from *c.*1913, was taken before the Nene Locks were modernised. When Peter Bonthron wrote about his journey down the Nene, in 1916, he noted, 'The lower locks on the route are well constructed and in better preservation than the others, having quite a modern appearance'.

113 Yarwell Lock, 1999. Working locks on the River Nene can be quite a strenuous process, as it requires many turns of a windlass to raise the guillotine gates. After a boat has locked through, a Nene lock should be left with the pointing doors shut and the guillotine gate raised. Yarwell Lock is another of the Nene Locks, which is 'reversed' at times of high water.

WANSFORD

114   The River Nene at Wansford was once the boundary between the Soke of Peterborough in Northamptonshire and the county of Huntingdonshire. Part of the village was in one county and part was in the other. Now, both are in Cambridgeshire. A stone bridge, connecting the two, was erected in the 16th century to replace a timber construction. Wansford Bridge originally had 13 irregular arches, built at various times, but the south side was damaged in an ice flood in 1795, and the arches were cut down to 10 during reconstruction. A datestone of 1795, on one of the arches, is a reminder of this time.

115   In past times, the Great North Road crossed the Nene on the grey stone bridge at Wansford. Now, the A1 by-passes the village. The soldiers pictured on this old postcard, dating from the First World War, may have been making for Wansford railway station, two miles to the south east of the village. At the further end of the bridge is St Mary's Church, noted for its 14th-century spire and carved Norman font.

116 The *Haycock Hotel* is situated at the southern end of Wansford Bridge and has a datestone of 1632. It was once an important coaching inn on the Great North Road between London and York. Its name is derived from an old story concerning 'Drunken Barnaby', who fell asleep on a stack of hay by the riverside. While he slept, the river rose and carried the haycock a little way downstream to the bridge. On awakening, the bemused Barnaby asked people on the bridge where he was, as he thought that he must have travelled some distance on the flood. When they told him Wansford, he queried, 'What, Wansford in England?' This addition to the name of the village has stuck since that occasion, though the tale has a number of variations.

117   A flood laps up to the foot of the bridge in this early 20th-century view of Wansford's main street. Transport through the flood is by horse and by punt. A pig, making its way through the flood water, adds interest to the scene.

118   This Edwardian view of the cross roads at Wansford shows cyclists walking up the slope of the Great North Road from Wansford Bridge. In the background is the Nene, while on the right is the wall of the *Old Mermaid* public house. Mrs. Harriet Ann Marshall was the proprietress of the latter in 1903. It was pulled down around the time of the Second World War to facilitate road improvement.

119 The Great North Road or A1 now crosses the River Nene on this concrete bridge, which dates from 1929. On one side of the central arch, in large capital letters, are the words COUNTY OF SOKE OF PETERBOROUGH, while on the other side COUNTY OF HUNTINGDON is inscribed.

120 The back of this old postcard indicates that Jenny, Miles, Rupert and David, the young people pictured, spent a day out boating on the River Nene at Wansford in 1924. A fifth member of the boating party, wearing a peaked cap, is holding the boat tiller. He may have been hired to steer the boat.

SIBSON

121   These cottages are next to Wansford station, which is now the headquarters of the restored Nene Valley Railway. In days past, they housed families whose menfolk worked on the railway. At the time of the 1881 census, the inhabitants included four railway signalmen, a railway pointsman and a platelayer on the L & N Railway. This photograph of Station Cottages is likely to have been taken during the first decade of the 20th century. Wansford station is nearer Sibson than Wansford, though Stibbington is the present-day postal address of the railway station.

122   Wansford station, 2001. The original station building is on the left-hand side of this view. A new station has been erected, on the opposite side of the track, to serve the restored Nene Valley Railway. The latter has a seven-and-a-half-mile line, which, in the main, follows the River Nene to Peterborough, passing through the 500-acre Ferry Meadows Country Park, where there is a station. Another station is at Orton Mere. The terminus of the line at Peterborough is a 10-minute walk from the city centre.

WATER NEWTON

123   Lock and mill, *c*.1910. Water Newton is picturesquely situated on the bank of the River Nene. At the time of the Domesday survey, there were three water mills here. The mill in the background of this view dates from 1791, though there were 19th-century alterations to the building. Charles J. Sampson was a miller and farmer at Water Newton in 1881. In the census of that year, three other inhabitants of Water Newton gave their occupations as corn millers. The mill was converted into five private residences in 1986. The traditional balance beams of the lock gates can be seen on the left-hand side of the picture. This lock was replaced by a lock of the guillotine type in the 1930s.

124   The church at Castor is dedicated to St Kyneburgha, the daughter of the Saxon King Penda of Mercia, who is said to have founded a convent of nuns here, *c*.650, on the site of a large Roman palace. It was consecrated on 17 April 1124. Standing in an elevated position, looking over the Nene valley, the Norman church has a central tower topped by a pyramidal steeple. Inside, there are a number of noteworthy features, including Saxon and Norman stone carvings and a wall painting showing scenes from the life of St Catherine. The wooden ceiling of the nave is decorated with angels. An interesting inscription on the tenor bell reads, 'To the Church the living call and to the grave do summon all. Henry Bagley made me 1700'.

125 Castor's *Royal Oak* inn is pictured here. In 1849, Elizabeth Smith was victualler of the *Royal Oak*, while Thomas Hill Smith was innkeeper there in 1881 and in 1890. Other 19th-century inns were the *George & Dragon* and the *Fitzwilliam Arms*. The latter commemorates the name of the Fitzwilliam family, owners of nearby Milton Hall. This was the seat of George Charles Wentworth-Fitzwilliam in the late 19th century.

ALWALTON

126   In this Edwardian view, the river and woodland at Alwalton Lynch look idyllic. Then, it was a favourite location for young couples, who were 'walking out' together. The tall trees, on the left, no longer stand, but the wooded cliff on the right is still eye-catching. In the vicinity of Alwalton Lynch, a hard blue shelly limestone, known as Alwalton Marble, was worked from the Roman era. In medieval times, it was used to decorate churches.

127   The staunch, Alwalton Lynch. When the River Nene was made navigable in the 18th century, besides locks, a number of staunches were used, which were employed to control the differences in water levels. The Nene staunches are likely to have been reconstructed in the 1830s by Thomas Atkinson. At Alwalton Staunch, a datestone of 1837 bore the initials T.A. The staunch was of the guillotine type and its side walls were constructed of large blocks of masonry, which sloped down from the gate. Other staunches on the Nene were at Wellingborough, Stanwick, Thorpe, Barnwell, Perio, Elton, Wansford, Orton and Woodston.

MILTON FERRY

128   The three-arched Milton Ferry Bridge is said to cross the Nene at the site of the former Gunwade Ferry. It was constructed in 1716 by Earl Fitzwilliam, who owned nearby Milton Abbey. The latter mansion was erected in the reign of Henry VIII, by Sir William Fitzwilliam, and is now known as Milton Hall. Ferry Lodge, which can be seen at the end of the bridge, was one of the entrances to Milton Hall and its park.

ORTON STAUNCH

129   An Edwardian boating party photographed at Orton Staunch. In past times, progress upriver in this locality could be slow, as boats had to wait for a head of water to build up, between staunches, before they could proceed. It was noted in *Bradshaw's Canals and Navigable Rivers* (1928) that the numerous staunches on the river below Wellingborough were a great hindrance to the navigation.

130 Orton Staunch, *c.*1920s. The staunch and its adjacent house, in the middle of the river, were demolished when Orton Lock was built in 1939 by the Nene Catchment Board. Orton Lock is still known locally as Orton Staunch.

WOODSTON

131 During August 1912, a wooden walkway was used by pedestrians and cyclists to pass over the flood at Oundle Road. This postcard memento of the occasion shows that the sight of high-wheeled horse-drawn traffic, attempting to get through, had attracted a number of onlookers.

PETERBOROUGH

132 This engraving entitled 'S.W. View of the City of Peterborough' dates from 1827. The cathedral dominates the skyline, while the church of St John the Baptist is shown to be much smaller. On the left of the view, a horse is towing a boat along the River Nene. Stone and other building materials were transported by water during the construction of the cathedral. It is thought that the stone barges, used in medieval times, may have been about 28ft. long and capable of carrying cargoes of about eight tons.

133 The West Front of Peterborough Cathedral was erected in the early 13th century. The cathedral is dedicated to St Peter, St Paul and St Andrew. Figures representing these saints stand at the apex of the three gables. The central porch, in the Perpendicular style, was added in the 14th century. In monastic times, the magnificent building was Peterborough Abbey and, after the Dissolution of the Monasteries, the abbey became Peterborough's cathedral. Today, it is celebrated for its Romanesque architecture and the unique painted ceiling in the nave, which dates from *c.*1220.

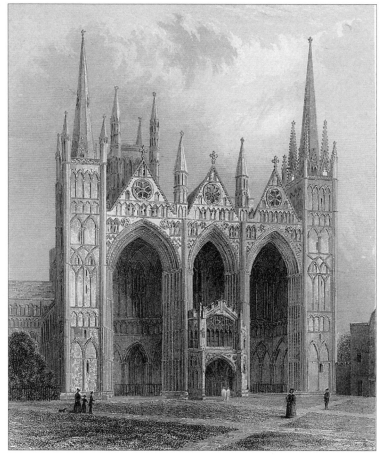

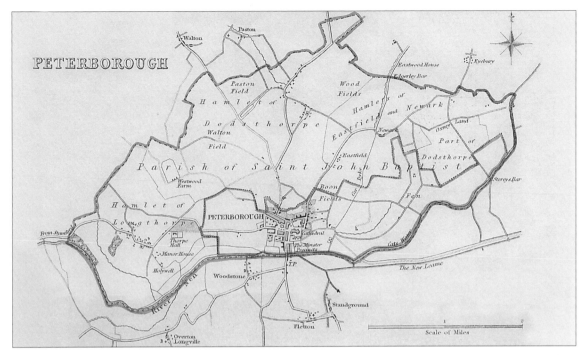

134 Map of Peterborough showing the River Nene on the southern edge of the city, c.1835. Before the coming of the railways, the River Nene was an important highway for Peterborough and its neighbourhood. *Pigot & Co.'s Directory* of 1823-4 had an entry under 'Water Conveyance' for Simpson, Mewburn and Miller's Boats, which left Peterborough for Wisbech every Tuesday and Friday morning at ten, returning on Wednesday and Sunday morning at eight. An entry in the Wisbech directory, for the same years, was less optimistic, noting that the Nene Packet left Wisbech for Peterborough every Wednesday and Sunday at nine, weather permitting.

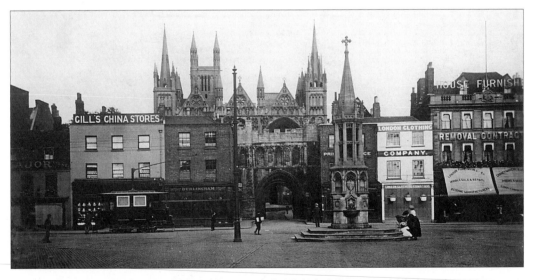

135 This view of the Market Place looks towards St Nicholas' Gateway, which dates from Norman times. The west front of Peterborough Cathedral soars behind it. To the left of the gateway is Gill's China Stores and Burlingham's shop, while to the right of it are the premises of printer, bookseller and stationer, George C. Caster, the London Clothing Company and the London Furnishing Company. In the foreground is the Gates Memorial water fountain, which had four taps and basins. This was put up in 1898 to commemorate Henry Pearson Gates, who was Mayor of Peterborough three times during the last quarter of the 19th century. Much has changed since this view was taken, c.1914. The Market Place has been re-named Cathedral Square and the memorial has been removed.

136 In the mid-19th century, markets in Peterborough were held for livestock on Wednesdays and for live and dead stock and general produce on Saturdays. Markets continued to be held in the Market Place until 1963. This bustling scene dates from the first decade of the 20th century. The arcaded Guildhall was built in 1671, probably on the site of an earlier building. The latter, formerly known as the Market Cross or Butter Cross, was used as Peterborough's Town Hall between 1874 and 1933. Behind the Guildhall is the parish church of St John the Baptist, which was erected in the early 15th century.

137 The junction of the Market Place and Long Causeway, *c.*1910. A double-decker open-topped tram appears to be obligatory in old postcard views of street scenes such as this. Peterborough's electric trams came into operation in 1903 and this service lasted until 1930. The advertisement on the tram is for Barrett's, the department store at the corner of Long Causeway and Midgate.

138 As its name implies, Narrow Bridge Street, leading off the Market Square, was not very wide, being only about 20ft. across. The *Angel* was at the corner with Priestgate, an inn by this name having been on this site for over 500 years. In the past, it was the venue for both private and public occasions, plus sporting events such as cock fighting. An advertisement from 1903 boasted that it had a 'large hall, handsomely decorated, for concerts, balls, dinners, wedding breakfasts and public meetings'. At that time, Joseph Clifton was the proprietor. Premises on the left, in the first decade of the 20th century, included that of bookseller and stationer, E.A. Hooke, where there was a circulating library. Around 1929, Narrow Bridge Street was widened by the demolition of its eastern side. The former Narrow Bridge Street and Broad Bridge Street are now known together as Bridge Street.

139 On the extreme right of this early 20th-century view of Town Bridge, a Fenland lighter is being loaded. People on the bridge are watching the activity. Prominent at the bow of the lighter is the 'sprit' or steering pole. In the background, looking north from the river, is Broad Bridge Street, with the *Boat Inn* and the *Rose and Crown Inn* on the left and the *Golden Lion Hotel* at the junction with Narrow Bridge Street in the distance.

140 A wooden bridge, on stone piers, was erected across the Nene in the early 14th century. This existed until 1872, with many renovations over the centuries. It was replaced by the iron Town Bridge, which, in turn, was superseded by a reinforced-concrete bridge, opened in 1934. When this early 20th-century photograph was taken, the people thronging the bridge were watching the boating activities on the river. Regattas were held on the Nene, at Peterborough, on the August Bank Holiday.

141 In August 1912, floods swept the country nationwide. At the peak of the flood, the River Nene rose to a height of 17ft. 6 in. on 27 August 1912, after 13½ hours of ceaseless rain the previous day. Crowds gathered on Town Bridge to watch the Nene's flood waters swirling past. This photograph shows that the river was almost to the top of the arches of the bridge. A Fenland lighter is in the foreground, riding high on the swollen waterway.

142 A variety of craft, including Fenland lighters and rowing boats, are moored downstream of Town Bridge in this photograph taken *c.*1914. On the north bank is the 18th-century Custom House, topped by a cupola, while on the south bank is the Midland Railway Company's Grain Warehouse No.1. Over the years, the railways took trade away from the river. An outline of transport on the Nene, in the late 1920s, was given in *Bradshaw's Canals and Navigable Rivers*. It stated that there was 'very little trade done on the river between Northampton and Peterborough', but that 'Fen lighters trade up to Wansford for stone'. In those days, before the improvements of the 1930s, the Nene was tidal up to Peterborough. However, the tide only gave enough depth of water between the city and Wisbech for 'the passage of loaded lighters on about five days in a fortnight'. Even then, lighters had to be frequently helped over the Northey gravel shoal, between Peterborough and Dog-in-a-Doublet, by the release of water from Woodston and Orton staunches, upstream of Peterborough.

DOG-IN-A-DOUBLET

143 Dog-in-a-Doublet Lock, 2000. The electrically operated Dog-in-a-Doublet Lock, with its huge guillotine gates, was constructed in the late 1930s by the Nene Catchment Board. Its adjoining sluice was built to control the high tides, which used to surge upstream towards Peterborough, threatening to flood parts of the city. The sluice ensures that the water level upstream is of sufficient depth for the passage of boats. The lock's curious name is also the name of the nearby riverside inn. It is said to have derived from the terrier, owned by a former innkeeper. The tale goes that the dog had lost its coat because of a skin complaint, so he wore a little leather jacket and became known as the 'Dog-in-a-Doublet'.

THORNEY

144 Thorney Abbey was among the greatest of the Benedictine abbeys in the country, before the Dissolution of the Monasteries. A magnificent church had been erected during Norman times. Most of this was destroyed, along with the extensive monastic buildings, when the abbey was suppressed during the reign of Henry VIII. While much of the stone was carried away for building elsewhere, the nave of the abbey, with its aisles removed, was eventually formed into the parish church, which still stands today. The west front with its twin stair turrets is depicted on this print, which dates from 1802.

WHITTLESEY

145 The late 17th-century Butter Cross, with its pyramidal roof of Collyweston slates, is the focal point of Whittlesey's Market Place, bringing to mind the town's history as a centre for agriculture. In the past, the ancient agricultural tradition of Straw Bear Dancing took place in Whittlesey, the origins of which are probably connected with corn gods of pagan times. This Fenland custom—of a man, dressed in straw, dancing through the streets on the Saturday before Plough Sunday—was revived in January 1979.

146 Whittlesey used its waterway to transport agricultural produce from the Fens. Ashline Lock is situated between King's Dyke and Whittlesey Dyke on the Nene-Ouse Navigation Link, which passes through Whittlesey, March, Outwell and Upwell. This photograph of the lock was taken c.1904. The present-day lock has recently been lengthened, so that longer craft may use the Fen waterways.

GUYHIRN

147   At Guyhirn, the Nene flows high above the village, behind huge banks. Along the road to Wisbech St Mary, which is parallel to the river, is Guyhirn's Puritan Chapel of Ease, built in 1660 at the end of the Commonwealth era. Its design is plain and simple and a delight to the eye. The chapel was restored in the 1970s and is maintained by the Churches Conservation Trust. Services no longer take place there.

148   In this view, which probably dates from before the First World War, a cluster of women and children stand outside Guyhirn's brick-built Primitive Methodist Chapel. The chapel stood opposite the high river bank. It does not exist today.

MARCH

149 The Old River Nene is part of the Nene-Ouse link. It flows through March to Marmont Priory Lock, before connecting with Well Creek, an eight-mile-long canalised river, which flows through Upwell and Outwell. At the end of the Well Creek is Salters Lode Lock, which leads to the tidal River Ouse. Winding through the centre of March, the Old River Nene is regarded in present-day tourist literature as being the 'town's finest asset'. There are certainly some picturesque buildings on its river frontage and convenient moorings for visiting holiday boats. This view shows the Old Nene from the bridge at the north end of the town, *c*.1917.

150 Children outnumber the adults in this High Street scene, dating from the early years of the 20th century. Markwell's shop, selling shirts, collars, ties, braces, hats and caps, is on the left. Further down the street, on the opposite side, is *Ye Olde Griffin*, one of the main inns of the town, now known as the *Griffin Hotel*. Out of view, High Street continues over the town's bridge to Broad Street on the north side of the river.

UPWELL

151 Upwell is intersected by the canalised section of river known as Well Creek. Its houses extend to Outwell on both sides of the waterway. In this view, dating from *c.*1910, St Peter's Church, a mainly Perpendicular building of Barnack stone, is in the background. A Fenland lighter is on the inside bend of the river.

152 Roads run on either side of Well Creek and the setting is reminiscent of a canal village in Holland. When this view was taken, *c.*1907, the houses on Upwell's west bank, in Cambridgeshire, faced those on the east bank in Norfolk, the river dividing the two counties. Now both sides of the waterway are in Norfolk.

OUTWELL

153 Outwell Lock on the Wisbech Canal, *c.*1908. The Wisbech Canal was a five-and-a-quarter-mile stretch of waterway between Wisbech and Outwell, linking the River Nene with Well Creek. It was begun in the late 18th century and abandoned in 1926. The last cargo, comprising 18 tons of straw, was taken through in 1922 by Vic Jackson, on behalf of Ellis & Everard. Outwell Lock, at the entrance to the canal, was completed in 1795 and measured 97ft. by 11ft. 6in., though only boats of up to 10ft. 10 in. width could use it.

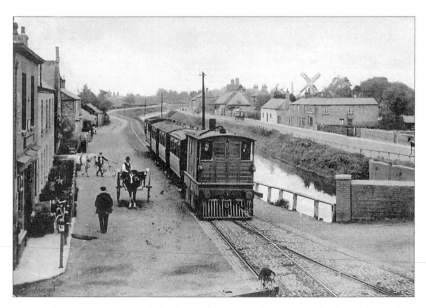

154 Steam tram, *c.*1908. A single-track tramway, between Wisbech and Upwell, was opened to Outwell in 1883 and to Upwell in 1884. Much of the track ran parallel to the Wisbech Canal. Inevitably, the tramway took away trade from the canal, tolls of which fell steeply after the coming of the steam trams. The closure of the canal happened first, while the tramway closed in 1966.

WISBECH CANAL

155   This is a rare photograph of a gang of Fenland lighters on the Wisbech
Canal during the early years of the 20th century. In the background of this
view is Wisbech Sluice, which had both navigation gates and sea gates. The
short stretch of tidal water, between the sluice and the canal's junction with
the River Nene, used to get silted up, causing problems for traffic on the canal.

WISBECH

156 Wisbech has a wealth of waterside buildings. North Brink and South Brink, which stretch along the River Nene, are noted for their elegant Georgian houses. Those on North Brink have particularly impressive facades, with no two being alike. The latter Brink is said to be among the finest Georgian streets in the country. However, although the buildings are very English in appearance, the riverside setting is reminiscent of the Netherlands. This photograph, looking towards the town's former iron bridge, was taken *c.*1912. A gang of Fenland lighters is just discernible below the bridge.

157 The tall Clarkson Memorial, in the foreground of this photograph, was designed by the architect, Sir George Gilbert Scott. It was erected in 1881 and commemorates a native of Wisbech, Thomas Clarkson (1760-1846). He was in the forefront of the movement for the abolition of slavery in the early years of the 19th century. The larger-than-life-size figure of Thomas Clarkson is holding a set of open manacles, symbolising the struggle against slavery. Peckover House, built in 1722 on North Brink, is in the middle distance. Formerly called Bank House and once the property of the banker, Jonathan Peckover, it is one of the outstanding features of Wisbech. This Georgian town house and its delightful gardens are now owned by the National Trust.

158   A single-span bridge, erected in 1857, replaced a graceful, but steeply humped stone bridge, which had been built in 1748. Intended as a swing bridge, though it didn't function as such, the iron bridge was, in its turn, replaced in 1931 by the present Town Bridge. Lilian Ream, a well-known Wisbech photographer, produced this postcard of the new bridge. Having established her own studio in 1909, she worked until 1949 and died in 1961 at the age of 84 years. During her long life, she compiled a considerable collection of photographic images, which recorded local people, places and special events. Several of these photographs are now in the Lilian Ream Exhibition Gallery collection, which is accommodated in the Tourist Information Centre in Bridge Street.

159   The name, Old Market Place, implies that it was once the town's centre of market trading before being superseded by the present-day Market Place, though this is debatable. Certainly it was an important business centre in the 19th century. Bordering the triangular area of the Old Market are some fine Georgian buildings, which have interesting architectural details. However, visitors to Wisbech today would look in vain for the Octagon Church, once an imposing feature in the Old Market. The church, which dated from 1826, was pulled down in the early 1950s. The rails, on the right of this photograph, were used by a light railway running through the port.

160 The draining of the Fens, which provided rich agricultural land, much increased Wisbech's trade as a market town. In the 1920s, when this view of the Market Place was taken, flowers and fruit were among the produce grown in the surrounding area. Other crops included potatoes, asparagus and mustard seed. The Market Place is spacious and traditional markets are still held here twice weekly, on Thursdays and Saturdays.

161 This view of High Street, taken *c.*1911, looks towards the Market Place. On the right, Woodman's cycle shop is next to Brenner's Bazaar, while on the left, at the end of the street, is the 19th-century brick facade of the *Rose and Crown Hotel*, one of Wisbech's oldest inns. An earlier inn, known as the *Pheasant and Horn*, once occupied the site. High Street, like the Market Place, has now been pedestrianised.

162 The oldest part of the church of St Peter and St Paul dates from Norman times, but rebuilding took place in the Middle Ages. A striking feature of the large church is that it has two naves and two chancels, making the width of the building almost the same as its length. Erected between *c*.1520 and 1530, the tower of the church replaced a west tower, which had collapsed. Unusually, the tower is linked to the northern side of the church.

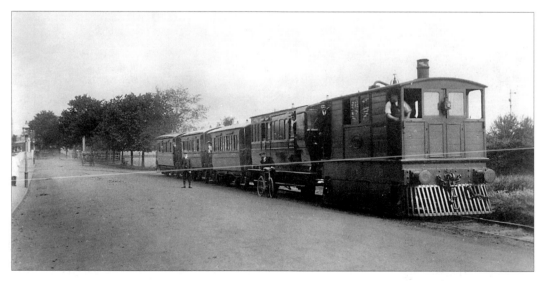

163 The steam tram, which once ran between Wisbech and Upwell, was a favourite subject for postcard publishers. Here it is pictured at Elm Road, on a postcard dating from before the end of the First World War. According to the authors of *Branch Line To Upwell* (1995), the locomotive in this view had brown woodwork and blue metalwork. Brake Van No.16 was behind the locomotive, followed by three tramcars. The six-mile journey between Wisbech and Upwell had originally taken one hour in 1884, but by 1902 this was reduced to 50 minutes and by 1907 it took 39 minutes. Between 1884 and 1902 the fare was 4d. for a first-class ticket, but by 1922 it had risen to 10d. The passenger service ceased in 1927.

164 This tranquil scene of lighters on the river and warehouses at Nene Quay dates from *c*.1920. The old brick-built warehouses were similar to those of the Hanseatic towns with which Wisbech used to trade. Those on the left bank had entrances on the riverside. Now, only one of the warehouses remains standing. Its opposite neighbour, on Nene Quay, was once the warehouse of Horace Friend, a dealer in metal, feathers, fur and skins. Both have now been converted into apartments. In the far distance, the former Mills' Brewery can be seen. Nowadays, the modern Freedom Bridge crosses the river near the Magistrates Court, which is built on the site of the brewery.

165   Old photographs of sailing ships at the town quays bear witness to the fact that Wisbech was once a busy port. Even before the 19th-century improvements to the river, it appears that Wisbech carried on a good trade by water. In 1791, it was noted in *The Universal British Directory* that the river was navigable at spring tides, which flowed there from six to eight feet, for vessels that drew 10 or 12 ft. of water. A considerable number of these craft of about 60 or 80 tons burthen were constantly employed in the corn-trade to places like London and Hull.

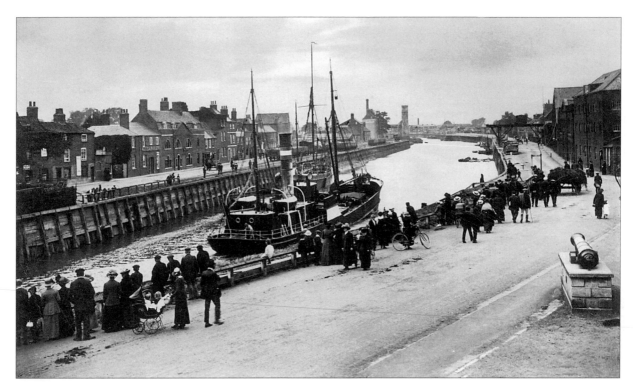

166   Boats on the river caused these Wisbech folk to stop and survey the scene, when this photograph was taken *c.*1918. Today, the town is attracting recreational boats to its quays by providing pontoon moorings and good facilities for both sea-going and river-using craft.

167   The port of Wisbech, 1912. Much timber from the Baltic was imported through Wisbech over the years. In this photograph, taken by Lilian Ream, a ship is being unloaded and there is a stack of timber on the quay. Two Fenland lighters are moored in front of the ship. Across the river, there is a line of trucks on the light railway through the port, which had a link with the Midland and Great Northern railway line. In the extreme right foreground, railings run alongside the Wisbech Canal, which is out of view.

168   A Baltic ship is moored at the quay in this early 20th-century view of the port of Wisbech. The timber on the quayside would have been unloaded by hand. Nowadays, although the shipping trade has much lessened, the quays downriver of Wisbech can cope with ships of up to 2,000 tonnes.

SUTTON BRIDGE

169 The Cross Keys swing bridge, viewed from the railway station on the Spalding to King's Lynn line, *c.*1909. This is the third bridge at Sutton Bridge. Sir John Rennie was the designer of the first bridge, erected in 1830. His oak-built structure had a 52-ft.-long central section, which was made of cast iron and could be moved. Robert Stevenson designed its replacement in the 1850s. The second bridge was erected a little way to the south of its predecessor and had a movable section, which was more than twice as long as that of the first bridge. The designer of the third bridge was J. Allen McDonald. Originally, this swing bridge, opened in 1897, carried both the Midland & Great Northern railway line and a road across the Nene. Now, only the A17 crosses the river, by the Cross Keys Bridge, the railway having closed in the late 1950s.

170 This aerial view of Sutton Bridge, dating from *c.*1923, shows the swing bridge over the Nene and a Thames barge on the river. To the left of the bridge, on the Lincolnshire side of the river, is the wharfage, while to the right is the railway station. St Matthew's Church, built in the Early English style in 1843, is in the foreground. It is said to be the only church, built of flintstone in Lincolnshire. Across the river, on the Norfolk bank, is flat agricultural land.

171 Swing Bridge, 2000. During recent years, the swing bridge has opened on average about three times a week to let ships pass to and from the port of Wisbech, which is about eight miles upriver of Sutton Bridge. In busier days, it used to open around 900 times a year.

172 New docks covering an area of 12 acres were opened at Sutton Bridge in 1881, but unfortunately these gave way in the same year. At the end of the 19th century, there was a good quay on the riverside and warehouses for corn, coal and timber at this location. However, by the 1920s, decline had set in along the wharfage, as the river was in a poor condition.

173 Port Sutton Bridge, 2001. In recent years, docks in this locality have been revived and are now known as Port Sutton Bridge. The modern port covers 62 acres and has a wharfage 350 metres long. The latter can accommodate four or five sea-going vessels of up to 120 metres in length at a time. Port Sutton Bridge handles dry cargoes such as steel, timber and agricultural products.

RIVER NENE OUTFALL

174   The East Lighthouse was once occupied by the naturalist, Sir Peter Scott. It is one of a pair of tall white towers situated on either side of the River Nene near Sutton Bridge, which look like lighthouses, though it is thought that they never carried lights. They are said to have been constructed as living accommodation for workers around the time the new outfall cut was being made for the river in 1830. John Seymour, in *Sailing through England* (1956), described the lighthouses as 'expressions of the exuberance of the Victorian engineers who planned the cut'. The Peter Scott Walk, following the seabank between Sutton Bridge and West Lynn, takes present-day walkers near to the outfall of the Nene.

175   Iris Wedgwood, in *Fenland Rivers*, wrote of the Nene making a 'discouraged arrival' at the Wash. However, on a summer's day, when the tide is in and the only sounds are those of sea birds and the breeze rippling through the tall grass, the Nene's outfall to The Wash is a serene end to a journey, which has covered around 91 miles from Northampton to the sea.

Bibliography

Abel, Derek and Thurman, Dorothy, *Wisbech – forty perspectives of a Fenland town* (1998)

Andrews, William, *Bygone Northamptonshire* (1891)

Bates, H.E., *Down the River* (1937)

'BB' (Watkins-Pitchford, Denys), *A Summer on the Nene* (1967)

Blagrove, David, *Waterways of Northamptonshire* (1990)

Blair, Andrew Hunter, *The Middle Level* (1999)

Bonthron, P., *My holidays on inland waterways: 2000 miles cruising by motor boat and pleasure skiff on the canals and rivers of Great Britain* (1916)

Bowden, Kim and Rayner, David, *Wisbech*, The Archive Photographs Series (1996)

Bowskill, Derrick, *The Norfolk Broads and Fens* (1999)

Boyes, John and Russell, Ronald, *The Canals of Eastern England* (1977)

Brandon, David and Knight, John, *Peterborough Past* (2001)

Brown, Cynthia, *Northampton 1835-1985* (1990)

Bull, June and Vernon, *Peterborough, A Portrait in Old Picture Postcards* (1988)

Bunch, Allan, *Peterborough in old picture postcards* (1996)

Bunten, Judy and McKenzie, Rita, *The Soke of Peterborough: A Portrait in Old Photographs and Picture Postcards* (1991)

Burman A., *Northampton in the Making: Part 1 The Changing Scene* (1988)

Butler, Mia, *Exploring the Nene Way* (1992)

De Salis, Henry Rodolph, *Bradshaw's Canals and Navigable Rivers: A Handbook of Inland Navigation* 3rd edn. (1928)

Evans, H.A., *Highways and Byways in Northampton & Rutland* (1918)

Gray, Allen, *Islip, Northamptonshire* (1993)

Greenall, R.L., *A History of Northamptonshire* (2nd edn 2000)

Greenall, R.L., *Daventry Past* (1999)

Guest, Clive and Swift, Andrew, *Wellingborough on old picture postcards* (1999)

Healy, John M.C., *The Last Days Of Steam In Northamptonshire* (1989)

Hill, Peter, *Around Oundle and Thrapston* The Archive Photographs Series (1997)

Humphries, Eric and Mary, *Woodford Juxta Thrapston* (1985)

Imray, Laurie, Norie and Wilson, *Map of the River Nene* (1999)

Ireson, Tony, *Northamptonshire* (1954, new edn 1964)

Islip Parish Council, *Islip Past And Present* (1995)

Jenkins, H.J.K., *Along the Nene* (1991)

Kelly's Directory of Northamptonshire (1890, 1903, 1914)

Mitchell, Vic, Smith, Keith, and Ingram, Andrew C., *Branch Line To Upwell* (1995)

Morris, John (gen. ed.), *Domesday Book: Northamptonshire* (1979)

Nicholson/Ordnance Survey, *Guide to the Broads & Fens* (1986)

Noble, Tony, *Northampton: A Guided Tour* (1989)

Northamptonshire Federation of Women's Institutes, *The Northamptonshire Village Book* (1989)

Northamptonshire Federation of Women's Institutes, *Within Living Memory* (1992)

Northamptonshire Industrial Archaeology Group, *A Guide to the Industrial Heritage of Northamptonshire* (2001)

Northampton Public Libraries, *Old Northampton* (1973)

Northamptonshire Libraries, *Life in Old Northampton* (1975)

Oswald, Arthur, *Old Towns Revisited* (1952)

Palmer, Joyce and Maurice, *Wellingborough Album* (1975)

Pearson, Michael, *Pearson's Canal Companion: Grand Union, Oxford, River Nene* (3rd edn. 1997)

Perrot, David, editor, *Nicholson/Ordnance Survey Guide to the Broads and Fens* (1986)

Perry, Stephen, *Peterborough A Second Portrait in Old Picture Postcards* (1989)

Pevsner, Nikolaus, *Northamptonshire*, The Buildings of England Series (2nd edn. 1973)

Pigot & Co.'s National Commercial Directory (1823-4, 1830, 1839, 1841)

Phillips, David, *The River Nene: From Source to Sea* (1997)

Post Office Directory of Northamptonshire (1877)

Powell, Roger and Bell, Robert, *Wisbech*, Britain in Old Photographs (1997)

Rice, Alan and Swift, Andrew, *Northamptonshire Railway Stations on old picture postcards* (1999)

Rotary Club of Oundle, *Old Oundle* (1985)

Rotary Club of Rushden, *Higham Ferrers – A Pictorial History* (1984)

Seymour, John, *Sailing through England* (1956)

Simper, Robert, *Rivers to the Fens* (2000)

Smith, Juliet, *Northamptonshire & The Soke of Peterborough: A Shell Guide* (1968)

St Peter's Parish Church, *Irthlingborough* (1988)

The Universal British Directory of Trade, Commerce and Manufacture (1791)

Wadenhoe History Group, *The Story of Wadenhoe* (1998)

Warren, Bill, *Thrapston: A Glimpse Into The Past* (1987)

Wedgwood, Iris, *Fenland Rivers* (1936)

Well Creek Trust, *Well Creek – The story of a waterway* (1983)

Whellan, William, *History, Gazetteer and Directory of Northamptonshire* (1849)

Whynne-Hammond, Charles, *Northamptonshire Place-Names* (1994)

Wisbech Official Guide, 1999

Leaflets

Cambridgeshire County Council Rural Group, *Nene Way: A Cambridgeshire Country Walk*
Dog in a Doublet, Whittlesey to Foul Anchor (1993)

Nene Valley Project, *Nene Way: A Northamptonshire County Path*
Southern Section: Badby to The Washlands
Central Section: Clifford Hill to Little Addington
Northern Section: Great Addington to Wansford

Northamptonshire Leisure and Libraries, *Nene Way: A Northamptonshire County Path*
Badby-Northampton Section (1988)

Northamptonshire Countryside Services, *Nene Way: A Northamptonshire County Path*
Northampton-Wellingborough Section 2 (1990)
Irchester-Thrapston Section 3 (1990)
Islip-Oundle Section 4 (1990)
Ashton-Wansford Section 5 (1990)

Peterborough City Council, *Nene Way: A Peterborough Country Walk*
Wansford – Dog in a Doublet (n.d.)

Index

Roman numerals refer to pages in the Introduction, and arabic numerals to individual illustrations